Mask Off

'Holds men accountable for the ways in which we benefit from male privilege, and liberates us from its violently toxic demands.'

David Lammy, MP

'JJ Bola knows that we have to find a new way forward. This book is good for all of us.'

Benjamin Zephaniah

'An uncompromising, heartfelt and completely vital interrogation of this thing we call masculinity. Bubbling with new perspectives and major insights – this is the book about masculinity that we ALL need.'

Jeffrey Boakye, author of *Black, Listed: Black British Culture Explored*

'Incisive, engaging, powerfully vulnerable, JJ Bola has given us an urgent and compelling examination of one of society's most pressing subjects.'

Musa Okwonga

Outspoken by Pluto
Series Editor: Neda Tehrani

Platforming underrepresented voices; intervening in important political issues; revealing powerful histories and giving voice to our experiences; Outspoken by Pluto is a book series unlike any other. Unravelling debates on feminism and class, work and borders, unions and climate justice, this series has the answers to the questions you're asking. These are books that dissent.

Also available:

Border Nation
A Story of Migration
Leah Cowan

Behind Closed Doors
Sex Education Transformed
Natalie Fiennes

Lost in Work
Escaping Capitalism
Amelia Horgan

Feminism, Interrupted
Disrupting Power
Lola Olufemi

Split
Class Divides Uncovered
Ben Tippet

Mask Off

Masculinity Redefined

JJ Bola

PLUTO PRESS

First published 2019 by Pluto Press
345 Archway Road, London N6 5AA

www.plutobooks.com

Copyright © JJ Bola 2019
By Agreement with Pontas Literary & Film Agency

The right of JJ Bola to be identified as the author of this work has
been asserted by him in accordance with the Copyright, Designs and
Patents Act 1988.

British Library Cataloguing in Publication Data
A catalogue record for this book is available from the British Library

ISBN	978 0 7453 3874 3	Paperback
ISBN	978 1 7868 0502 7	PDF eBook
ISBN	978 1 7868 0504 1	Kindle eBook
ISBN	978 1 7868 0503 4	EPUB eBook

This book is printed on paper suitable for recycling and made
from fully managed and sustained forest sources. Logging, pulping
and manufacturing processes are expected to conform to the
environmental standards of the country of origin.

Typeset by Stanford DTP Services, Northampton, England

Simultaneously printed in the United Kingdom and United States of
America

Contents

Acknowledgements

An acknowledgement and thanks to the Society of Authors for the grant award in support of me writing this book. For more information, please visit www.societyofauthors.org.

Thanks also to the 8 club by the Young Vic Theatre – the source of the testimonies used throughout the book. For more information, please visit: www.youtube.com/user/YoungVicLondon.

Introduction

Mask off: Being a man

One sunny Saturday afternoon during my teenage years, before touch screen and selfies, before 4G, before social media had permeated every aspect of our being, I was walking through the vibrant, often tumultuous, multicultural, dynamic Tottenham High Road in North London. I was with a large group with about ten, of my 'uncles'. They weren't really my uncles. They were not blood relatives, but the men who made up the Congolese community I had grown up in. On Saturdays, as part of their church group, they ran activities for young people in the community, which included the brass band music and other cultural activities.

After attending one of these Saturday sessions, I was invited for food at one uncle's house who lived locally, just off the high street. My excitement could not be contained. It was an unexpected treat of *pondu, makemba, mikate* and *ntaba* (stew, plantain, doughnut balls also known as puff puff, and grilled goat) – truly a privilege. We walked along the high street making our way to the house, chatting excitedly. I was noticeably the only teenager in the group, dressed in my tracksuit bottoms, hooded jumper and Nike Air Force 1 trainers. They were mostly dressed in the unique fashion of Congolese men: high-waisted jeans, colourful t-shirts fitted tight to unathletic, pot-belly type bodies, designer brands and eccentric designs.

As we walked, I began to feel very self-conscious and increasingly aware of the group I was with. Although I was very familiar with Tottenham – I spent a lot of time there as a teenager and had walked the same streets often, though with an entirely different group and a different purpose – I felt self-conscious because we were attracting a lot of attention, not just as a large group, but as a large group of eccentrically dressed men of African descent speaking loudly in Lingala. I also saw lots of other teenagers. Some began staring, pointing, and even laughing in the distance. I was certain some of them recognised me as I tried to hide by putting my hood up. In hindsight, this probably had the opposite effect.

We continued to walk through as a group, now split up in pairs or in threes, each holding their separate conversations. I walked with my uncle, holding hands. This is perfectly normal in Congolese/Francophone African culture, and I would later learn, in many other cultures around the world too. It is a way for men to bond and show affinity, as well as affection towards each other. This is the culture I had grown up in. I had often watched my father holding hands while speaking with other men in the community, or as they walked. It was normal, and in those situations I did not think twice of it. However, outside of the cultural norms of this group, it took on an alien and embarrassing quality.

Much to my relief, we turned off the high road, and walked towards the housing estate where the uncle who was hosting us lived. I had been to his house many times before. I wanted to run there on my own, ahead of the uncles, and wait there for them but the burden of explaining this behaviour would last with me much longer than I wanted or needed it too.

I was breathing a bit more relaxed and freely, though still walking hand in hand with my uncle. We were no longer in the direct gaze of all of those people on the street, particularly the teenagers. As we turned onto the estate where my uncle lived, with a renewed sense of vigour and boisterousness, a group of teenagers who were hanging out on the estate noticed us. They watched us; their eyes focussing on me and the uncle I walked hand in hand with. I could see their faces portraying a range of negative expressions, everything from confusion to disgust.

I had seen those youths on the estate before. Sometimes I'd even given them the subtle head-nod, an in-group greeting that comes with respect and acceptance. On these estates – and every estate, inner-city area, hood, ghetto, ends, slums, whatever the moniker – respect is all about how strong you are, or at least, how strong you are perceived to be. I had participated in this façade long enough to be granted respect. I was tall and athletic looking. Having had an early introduction to press ups and weights, I appeared just intimidating enough. All of this respect earned quickly dissipated before my very eyes, as I was seen walking hand in hand with another man.

I wanted to put my hood back on and bury my face but it was too late, I had already been seen. I quickly removed my hands from my uncles, pretending to reach for something in my pocket, which he seemed non-fussed about; another futile act.

'Yo, big man?' I heard a voice call over. I knew he was talking to me and no one else. I looked over. His eyes punched through my chest. I felt my legs shake as if my knees would buckle at any given step. He had his hood up over his head, and wore the grey Nike tracksuit and hoodie that was envied by all.

'You holding hands, yeah?' he said, and the crew around him chuckled, and exploded with laughter. I can still remember the pain; the sting in my heart. It is the same feeling from when spicy food goes from tasty to too hot to bear, and it makes you wish things could return to normal.

'No,' I replied, in a tone indicating that I was offended at the suggestion.

'*Alobi nini?*' My uncle, wondering what the commotion was about, asked what he had said.

'Nothing,' I replied with bitter disdain, 'he was asking for the time.'

* * *

This is one of the many experiences that I had growing up that made me question my masculinity, leading me to reflect on the question that we're not supposed to ask: what does it actually mean to be a man? Why was it that in one part of the world, two men holding hands did not turn any heads, yet in another part of the world everybody stopped and stared? I wondered about men's emotions and feelings, or rather, the apparent absence of it. I was quite an emotional boy. I cried if I was sad or upset; I cried if I was happy; I cried from anger. I expressed myself fully, whether that was through sadness or joyousness. But as I got older, this slowly changed. I become more stoical, more repressed, more reserved; I never let anyone else know how I truly felt, sometimes not even myself. There was a burning anger or rage inside that I disguised as anger issues, a short fuse or inability to control my temper.

Moving forward to the present day, what do our own perceptions of masculinity and the wider cultural norms around it mean for young boys growing up into manhood? What do they mean for young men and older men grappling with a society that encourages them to hold on to the anger that destroys the lives of women as well as the lives of many men? There are many urgent questions to consider about modern-day men and masculinity. Why are men overwhelmingly represented as perpetrators of violent crimes in statistics, particularly in regards to sexual violence, from harassment to rape? Why is suicide the biggest killer of men under the age of 45 – more than disease or accidents? What can we do to change this?

In order to gain a deeper understanding of the notion of being a man and masculinity, we have to understand patriarchy, which is the ideology and hierarchical structure that places men at an advantageous position above women, granting them power, privileges, entitlement, and access to resources in various domains and contexts: from within the family to business and the workplace, informing us of the roles that men and women should adhere to, while dictating their material realities. The expectation that women should cook and clean while men should be the primary wage earners is a rigid idea that may not hold the same weight and expectation as it did 50 years ago. But does that mean we live in an equal society? People may argue that women are liberated from such strict confines. On the surface, the image of the housewife is not as prevalent in our minds, but if women are still paid less than men in the same job, what does that tell us about how far we've come? As I discuss throughout the book, patriarchy is a thread that runs throughout the family, the education system, the mainstream media. It socialises men's behaviours, attitudes, and actions, telling them the way they should act, feel, and behave in all aspects of their lives, particularly in relation to women, as well as other men.

The system of patriarchy is something that impacts the lives of men and women, from birth through to childhood, adulthood and onwards, in sometimes seemingly simple ways such as the colours that they should wear, blue for a boy, pink for a girl, and the types of clothes or the toys that they should play with. These all have a significant impact on the way masculinity is viewed within society and how men and women interact with each other. A patriarchal society is a society in which men hold the primary stakes of power on a public level, for instance, in governance and politics, economics and business, education and employment, and religion, and on a private and interpersonal level, in the household, within relationships, and within friendships too. The patriarchy protects and prioritises the rights of men over the rights of women.

Patriarchy is not a term or system that many people are familiar with outside of academia, classrooms or textbooks. Nor is it used with frequency or in everyday regular conversation, although the conversation about feminism has been taking centre stage in recent years, resulting in a lot more exposure to the term. However, once a discussion gets going, it isn't difficult to get people to understand the notion of patriarchy, even if they haven't thought about it before, because it plays out in our everyday lives. The ways in which it does are the focus of this book.

I did not hear about patriarchy growing up. Not in school; not so much at university – at least not in a way that stood out to me – nor in my area or neighbourhood, on my block, among my male and female friends, in my family, and not from my parents, aunties, uncles, or siblings. It wasn't part of my everyday language – although I wish it had been as I would have been able to prepare myself for so many things. However, it did permeate virtually every aspect of my being and significantly influence the way I saw myself as a young boy, and later as a man, as well as the way that I saw other men and women. I recall being confronted with the ideas of male dominance in one form or another. For example, when I first heard the song 'Keep Ya Head Up' by Tupac Shakur, at approximately twelve or thirteen years old, in the late 90s/early 2000s. The following lyrics really struck me:

INTRODUCTION: MASK OFF: BEING A MAN

You know it makes me unhappy?

When brothers make babies, and leave a young mother to be
a pappy.

And since we all came from a woman,

Got our name from a woman, and our game from a woman,

I wonder why we take from our women, why we rape our
women,

Do we hate our women?

I think it's time to kill for our women, time to heal our
women,

Be real to our women.

And if we don't, we'll have a race of babies that will hate the
ladies

And makes the babies. And since a man can't make one, he
has no right

To tell a woman when and where to create one.

These lyrics are a commentary on aspects of gender inequality; on men who abandon women they've impregnated, men violating women, including rape, even asking 'do we hate our women?' Hearing this particular message from a gangster rapper who was firmly considered to be a masculine man; the epitome, of what a man should be, had a profound effect on my thinking as an adolescent.

When I did eventually come to understand the term patriarchy, it helped me to understand and make sense of the many questions I had as a young boy. For example, my curiosity about lyrics such as those above came to be understood within the wider context of women's reproductive rights. The same kind of questions, many boys still have growing up nowadays. Through my work with teenagers, as well as adult men, it seems we are still navigating the complexities and issues of being a man that were around decades ago, along with the new issues that have emerged in the modern day.

I have seen young boys, and men, quietly suffer with issues such as anxiety and depression, heartache and emotional trauma, lash out with aggression, at others and themselves, all because, repeatedly, somewhere along the line, they were told that a man has to be strong; tough, stoic, logical, a type of soldier in difficult times, never succumbing to emotion or vulnerability, always showing indifference to any kind of pain or suffering. And I too have learned from my experiences and the ways I have navigated issues around my masculinity and manhood, from the questions I had as a young boy, and teenager, and the questions that emerge as a man and how I have dealt with them, often in the very stereotypical form of male repression.

This is one of the reasons I decided to name this book *Mask Off*. Because men are taught to wear a mask, a façade that covers up how we are really feeling and the issues we are faced with from a young age. And because society is generally patriarchal, in that, it favours men that occupy privileged positions, it makes it seem as though men do not have issues that they are also suffering from. It is a kind of double-edged sword, a poisonous panacea; that is to say, the same system that puts men at an advantage in society is essentially the same system that limits them; inhibits their growth and eventually leads to their break down. The other reason for the title *Mask Off* is that it is a reference to the song, of the same title, by American rapper Future. The song is very hyper-materialistic, violent and misogynist, with braggadocios and lyrical references to drugs and money, gang-violence, and derogatory monikers for women (the b-word etc), all over a melodious flute sample. I later found out this is a sample from the original song by Tommy Butler called *Prison Song*, a song written for the play *Selma*. It captures the issues of racism, police brutality, and of love and freedom during the civil rights era. This contrast – two very different messages, over a span of time, existing in one song – is a very symbolic representation of how manhood and masculinity has changed over the years. And how it has been so deeply influenced by popular music and mainstream media.

With *Mask Off* my aim is to unmask the illusion of the rigid and limited masculinity that renders boys and men incapable of dealing with their emotions, and turns them into aggressors and dominators of other people, whether intentionally or otherwise, and to offer solutions as to how men can begin not only to heal from their own personal trauma and unlearn what they were taught as absolute, but also to make changes that will allow the next generation that are growing up to live in the fullness, fluidity and the wholeness of understanding of what being a man means.

Chapter 1

Real men: Myths of masculinity

If a man looks at masculinity as his spine, removing that spine does not make sense to him. – Rhael

There are several myths about masculinity that have been passed on to each generation as absolute truths. We have been taught it from a young age, almost without question, and any boy or man who does not fit into these stereotypical notions is virtually exiled from the male clan. It is as if being a man is a sports league that all men are trying to play in – the premier league being the elite league where only a few actually make it and belong – and the rest are in the lower leagues or the sub-divisions – the semi-professionals, the amateurs – while some are not in any league at all. The idea of being a man and the notions of masculinity that come with it more so resemble a sport that has ever-changing rules, depending on the location it's played in. Can you imagine if that were actually the case? If you play football in England, the rules are eleven a side and you kick the ball with your feet, but in America, when you play football (soccer), you're allowed to use your feet and hands. Move across the globe to Brazil, where you're only allowed to use your left foot, the goals are smaller, and there are 24 players on each team. In India the football isn't actually a football, but a watermelon that you kick around, and in Nigeria you're only allowed to use your head.

Manhood, much like masculinity, is not a fixed entity. It is not a square block that fits neatly into a square shaped hole in a square shaped world. It is ever changing, it is fluid, and more importantly, it is and can be anything you want it to be. However, as long as there remain rigid and stereotypical beliefs around masculinity that go unchallenged, men are often unable to subscribe to a masculinity that sits outside of the status quo. The list is endless – particularly as the prevalence of certain myths depends on which part of the world you are in. So, I've outlined nine prevalent myths around masculinity.

Real man

How often have you heard a phrase that sounded like *a real man takes care of his kids,* or *a real man doesn't cheat on his partner* or *a real man pays for everything* or anything else that starts with 'real man' (or 'real men') and then continues with a set of stipulations for a particular act? There is no such thing as a 'real man'. The phrase itself is actually based on patriarchal ideals that reinforce how men are expected to be. And in many cases, the context in which the phrase is used often says very little that is positive about manhood or being a man. Consider 'a real man takes care of his kids'. This is what you are *supposed to do* as a parent regardless of gender. The fact that only a 'real man' takes care of his kids inherently implies that the rest of men, generally, do not take care of their children, and so what does that have to say about men? The phrase 'real man' takes us back to the elite football league that men are supposed to play in: that only the 'real men' belong there. The idea of 'real men' being the providers or breadwinners is also based on material or financial

11

circumstances, and fails to account for social disadvantages and exclusion. These stereotypes work to reinforce limited notions of what a man can and cannot be: they are used in a number of contexts and can put a lot of pressure on men.

Men are trash

In recent years, this phrase came alive on the Internet, across social media, sparking a much needed conversation on male privilege and gender inequality, highlighting the systematic advantages that patriarchy affords men. It isn't (uniquely) about relationships or dating, although it is often reduced to that. Some retort this by saying 'choose better men' or deny its validity by the now infamous phrase 'not all men!' The 'trash' element does, understandably, trigger a defensive stance, which often comes from the misunderstanding that it is a personal attack on an individual, rather than a comment on the collective oppression of women. However, the defensiveness is also because people often become defensive when they are not ready to acknowledge the hurt they have caused in someone else's life. In many cases, the 'trashness' is simply a reference to men's abuse of their privilege, which occurs daily in society, whether men are aware of it or not. I was also taken aback when I first heard this phrase: it came across as bitter and even angry, but when I listened beyond the initial reaction or visceral emotion that it provoked, I understood that it told us more about societal issues around gender than it did about a particular man.

The nice guy/good guy

This idiom perpetuates male entitlement on an insidious level. While on the surface, it may appear to evoke a positive image of a man, the idea of a nice guy or good guy implicitly communicates that he is safe, and therefore entitled or deserving of women's attention, time, and labour. That women should like you if you are a nice guy, and if they don't, it reflects badly on the women in question. When men call themselves good guys, they are also subtly suggesting that men on the whole are so bad, that they have to distinguish themselves as different from the rest, often trying to find a way around the male privilege they have in common.

Man up

This phrase is often used as an emotional silencing tool, particularly towards boys in their childhood. Consider the following scenario: a young boy is playing outside and falls over, grazes his knee and begins to cry. He runs over to his parent who – quite often unknowing of the harmful effects it may have – tells them to 'man up', often followed by claims that boys are meant to be strong and so on. Boys quickly learn that expressing emotions, particularly displays of vulnerability such as crying, are weaknesses. And they internalise this, so that by the time they transition from boyhood through their adolescence to manhood, they suppress emotion internally without even realising it.

'That's gay'

This phrase is almost exclusively used when men share a form of (non-sexual) intimacy, express feelings or bonds in a way that goes beyond the hypermasculine expectations. It could be something simple like saying 'I love you.' Or two men hugging or holding hands. Whatever the expression, when it's between two men and brings them closer, it's usually perceived in this way. There is also the issue of men saying 'no homo' or 'pause', for the same reasons as above, instead of outwardly saying 'that's gay.' For example, men may say to one another: *you look really good today, no homo*. It's an insidious homophobic comment. Although it's generally used in jest, it nonetheless perpetuates a deep-rooted, toxic expression of masculinity: that if men care about one another, compliment one another, or show affection for one another, it needs to be qualified with the assertion that they are straight.

Men don't cry

This is virtually an extension of 'man up' that young boys carry through to adulthood. I can recall the first time, as a young boy, that I saw my father cry. It left me in shock. I had been told to be strong and not to cry all my childhood, and the one person who I saw as the ultimate source of strength was in tears in front of me. So, rather than figuring it was okay to cry, the conclusion I came to, as I grew into my adolescent years, was to make sure that I was strong enough – even stronger than my father – that no one would ever see me cry; no one would ever see my weaknesses. It took a long time to unlearn this thinking. I cry comfortably now, and in any space: after seeing a play at the theatre, during a concert, after losing a game of basketball or when I'm on my own. I even sneak a cheeky cry while chopping onions to cook, so I can get all my cries out at once. After several conversations, I realised that many of my adult male friends still do not feel comfortable with this level of vulnerability. I have male friends who say they have not cried in years, or they did not cry at all during a tragic moment; when a loved one passed or during a break up of a relationship, etc. Crying is also not reserved for negative moments alone; it can be an expression of lamenting and sadness, but it can equally deeply express overwhelming joy and happiness – don't you love it when you see a man cry on his wedding day – and both are perfectly valid.

Men are stronger than women

There is a video on YouTube, 'Labour Pain Simulator on 2 Men', where two men go to a doctor to have electrodes simulation on their abdomens to simulate the pain of labour for one hour. At first, the men are very nonchalant; one of them even says, 'as you know women exaggerate everything.' By the end of the process, they are both writhing in pain, unable to handle the simulated contractions. One man at the end calls his mother a superhero and hilariously apologises for putting her through this pain all those years ago. So often our views about strength, both physical and emotional, are linked to gender. There are of course biological differences between men and women, however, an absolutist approach to what those differences mean and how they play out in reality, are often rigid and flawed. Men are not by default stronger than women. Strength is a differential quality, often based on the situation (and not who can do the most press ups, lift the heaviest thing, hit the hardest or take the most hits). And arguably, the greatest strength of them all is emotional strength, rather than the physical; having the resilience to endure and overcome, and the capacity to recover quickly from adversity. If this is how we saw strength, would we be able to redefine who is stronger?

Men are logical (and women are emotional)

This phrase is often rooted in the desire to remove men from their emotional vulnerability and empathy for others. Men are considered to be the more logical gender, in that, supposedly, they think through their actions and decisions, judging each situation based on the best possible outcome, whereas women judge based on how they feel. What is often overlooked when we talk about the 'male logic', is other emotions, such as anger or rage. When domestic violence goes up by 40 per cent because a national football team has lost in an international competition, that kind of anger and aggression is certainly not the more logical.

Men have a higher sex drive/men think more about sex

There is a popular saying attributed to nineteenth century Irish poet and playwright, Oscar Wilde, which goes: 'Everything in the world is about sex except sex, sex is about power.' I first heard this quote as a teenager, and it struck me. It breaks down the projected male psyche in two parts; the first – 'everything is about sex except sex' – arguing that people act or perform in a way that increases the likelihood of them attracting a sexual mate. And the second part – 'sex is about power' – reflects how sex itself is often seen and enacted as a means to acquire domination over another person. That is why the idea of men having sex with multiple women is often celebrated in society; men are graciously labelled with epithets such as ladies' man, heartbreaker or player, while women are labelled as slut, slag, hoes, whore, j-bag, sket, and so forth. The list is endless. In truth, men and women have on average an equal amount of sex drive. Also, there are many men who do not feel fulfilled by having multiple partners and many women who do.

Honourable mention: 'boys will be boys'. This is arguably one of the most impactful idioms because it starts from a young age and sets boys onto a path where eventually, by the time they reach manhood, destructive behaviour patterns have been normalised. As children, 'boys will be boys' is often used to excuse the kinds of behaviour that are superficially associated with maleness – the kinds of behaviour that would not be accepted from a girl. It can be used when young boys are play-fighting – this phenomena almost exclusively happens among boys, often starting in school playgrounds – through to manhood, for example, through catcalling or sexual harassment. 'Boys will be boys' removes accountability from action, and teaches young boys that there are certain behaviours they can get away with as a result of their maleness – think about how there is no such equivalent of *girls will be girls*.

> One thing I don't like about gender roles is that men can't cry. We can get on the phone to our girlfriends and chat for like hours on end, and say this has happened etc, etc, that's our therapy. Our friends are our therapy, we've built that up over years but men, they don't have that because their boys will be like 'fam, fix up man, why you acting waste for,' and 'just get over it' . . . I think it's very important for men to be able to just express. – Zeze

There are many more examples of this kind of narrow-minded, limited thinking, which is actually used to reinforce a stereotypical perspective of what a man should and shouldn't be. This varies and differs depending on culture, location, and era – which only goes to show that masculinity is not fixed. Outward expressions of masculinity, including stereotypes of it, do not exist in a vacuum, but rather exist within society. By the time we as men become aware of some of these performed expectations, we will have already spent many years living up to it in one way or another through what we are told is 'normal', making it that much harder to unlearn.

Masculinity as performance

In the modern era, fierce debates are taking place around masculinity, femininity, and the gender binary itself – something we discuss in Chapter 6. Some argue that masculinity is toxic, fragile and in crisis, while others argue that increasing debate on it proves that masculinity is to be protected at all costs by those attempting to destroy it. Masculinity and femininity, as traditionally understood, are traits or characteristics that we exhibit on the basis of our sex, but it remains distinct from the definition of the male and female biological sex.

Judith Butler argues that 'gender is an identity tenuously constructed in time . . . through a stylised repetition of acts',[1] highlighting its performative nature. While gender is not the same thing as masculinity and femininity, gender *roles* largely tend to fit into masculine and feminine roles. Many have argued that this idea of gender as performative can be extended to masculinity and femininity: that we perform specific 'masculine' and 'feminine' roles and acts which continuously validate our sense of our gender: for example, being strong makes us more of a man, and being weak makes us more of a woman.

The many things that we are told about manhood and masculinity are actually dangerous to us, as boys and men, and to those who are close to us, including women – something that will be developed in further detail throughout the book. What are the examples, then, of how masculinity is different depending on location and culture in the world? We've already seen, a bit, an

---

1 Judith Butler, *Gender Trouble: Feminism and the Subversion of Identity* (New York and London: Routledge, 1990).

example of how in places like Nigeria, Uganda and India – and Congo, via my story in the first chapter – that men hold hands as a sign of brotherhood, friendship and affection. Throughout history there are various other examples, such as societies that are largely matriarchal and matrilineal – meaning societies where women held positions of power, and were not considered to be inferior, or weaker than men, and lineage and inheritance was passed on through the woman. That's not to say those societies manifested in the same way that a male-dominated or patriarchal society does in terms of oppressive structures: rather it means that their women were in positions of power and not rendered a marginalised group.

Feminist writer and researcher Heide Goettner-Abendroth argues that matriarchal societies should not be seen as mirror images of patriarchal ones; they do not have patriarchy's hierarchical definition. Matriarchal societies are socially egalitarian, economically balanced, and politically based on census decisions (democratic). They were created by women and founded on maternal values.[2]

There are still matrilineal societies around the world. For example, the Minangkabau ethnic group – the world's largest surviving matrilineal society – in West Sumatra, Indonesia, where land and property is inherited through the daughters, the children take their mother's name, and a man is considered a guest in his wife's home. It is a complex and distinct societal and political structure where women's agency is strengthened and empowered, rather than suppressed as in many places elsewhere in the world.[3]

---

2   Heide Goettner-Abendroth, *Matriarchal Societies: Studies on Indigenous Cultures Across the Globe* (Oxford: Peter Lang Publishing, 2012).

3   www.bbc.com/travel/story/20160916-worlds-largest-matrilineal-society (last accessed 22/11/2018).

Today, we are still caught up in the idea that the colour pink is for girls and blue is for boys (consider how popular internet gender reveal videos are), so it can be hard to imagine that make-up or high heels – 'feminine' things – were in some instances originally designed for men, or were things that men enjoyed. During the early seventeenth century, high heels were brought to Europe from Persia, and men typically wore high heels as a display of their upper-class status. The shoes were expensive, and so to wear them was to show that one had material wealth and financial status. Heels also made men look taller and more athletic. There is a famous portrait of King Louis XIV, of France, standing boldly in full-length tights, white shoes with a thick brown heel of approximately three inches.

Ultimately, masculinity is a performance; that is to say, it is acted out in a way that reinforces the widely held view of what is normal for those born as male. That's not to say that masculinity is in and of itself destructive – but there is of course, the issue of toxic or hegemonic masculinity, which is explored throughout the book. R. W. Connell argues that hegemonic masculinity is dangerous, because it 'legitimises powerful men's dominant position in society and justifies the subordination of the common male population and women, and other marginalised ways of being a man'.[4] When we consider that it is an ideal that has historically operated in a different way that is fluid and transformative across various cultures, we begin to see how it is not a stable force.

Masculinity is not patriarchy. And while patriarchy is an oppressive structure that imposes the dominance of one gender over another, we must imagine and manifest a masculinity that is not reliant on patriarchy to exist; a masculinity that sees the

4   R. W. Connell, *Masculinities* (Oakland: University of California Press; second edition, 2005).

necessity of the equality of genders for it to not only survive, but to thrive.

That's why I like talking about masculinities, rather than masculinity, because there are so many forms of it. We have an idea of masculinity and that becomes toxic or that becomes a negative stereotype, whereas masculinities allows any person be it man, woman, or gender non-conforming person to access their masculinities. – Tom

Chapter 2

Gang signs & prayer: Male violence, aggression and mental health

Male violence and aggression has a profound impact on our lives, the lives of our loved ones, and the lives of people we don't know. It ranges in intensity, but its toxic energy is often bubbling beneath the surface in many interactions and situations. We see the effects it has on households, in the workplace, in local communities and within society at large. However, despite its all-pervasive nature, much of male violence goes unseen – its more insidious elements in particular. Often, male violence is characterised as something natural – even second nature – for men. This is due to a lack of discussion about the root causes of male violence. We're used to hearing a repeated refrain about biology and testosterone. This tends to dismiss the vital factor of socialisation. Male violence and aggression is undoubtedly linked to male mental health. But we have yet to see widespread interventions, particularly for young men. We also don't have strategies in place for men of an older age, to unlearn toxic misogynistic attitudes and behaviour. Interventions and insight of this kind have the power to enable long-lasting change on the individual level, which could eventually cause a transformation on the collective societal level.

When it comes to the statistics, male violence is a minefield, from minor assault, all the way to murder. Sexual violence and aggression covers everything from rape to harassment and abuse, which may include no physical harm. According to the latest Office of National Statistics (ONS) Crime Survey for England Wales (CSEW, March, 2017) report on Violent Crime and Sexual offences, men were reported to be the perpetrators of 78 per cent of violent incidents. That is really close to four out of five of all violent crimes being committed by men. The CSEW also estimated that only 43 per cent of violent incidents were reported to the police. This is a significant reduction from estimated reports of 52 per cent from the year before. For the year ending March 2018, according to the CSEW, there were a total number of 1,259,000 violent crimes.

The findings also indicate that men are more likely to be victims of violent crime, with 2.1 per cent of males, compared with 1.3 per cent of females, 74 per cent of these being murders. However, women were more likely to be victims of violence against a person and violence without injury, reported at 53 per cent, and 57 per cent respectively. Women are more likely to experience violence within the household. This is often recorded as domestic violence, domestic abuse or intimate partner violence, rather than 'violent crime', so the statistics differ depending on the categorisation.[1]

The statistics on domestic violence are frankly shocking. In the year prior to March 2017, 1.9 million people (1.2 million women

---

[1] www.ons.gov.uk/peoplepopulationandcommunity/crimeandjustice/ compendium/focusonviolentcrimeandsexualoffences/yearendingmarch2016/ overviewofviolentcrimeandsexualoffences (last accessed 01/12/2018).

and 713,000 men) experienced domestic violence.[2] Two women a week are killed as a result of domestic violence in England by a partner or ex-partner. In the UK, in 2016, nine out of ten women killed knew their murderer. Research published by the United Nations Office on Drugs and Crime in 2018 stated that the home is the most dangerous place for a woman.[3] For many people, it is inconceivable that the place you are most likely to be attacked, abused or even murdered is in your home – a place that many people consider to be their safe space – and for the crime to take place at the hands of a person known to the victim.

Statistics reveal men commit the overwhelming majority of violent crimes: almost 80 per cent. However, less than half of these crimes are reported to the police. They also reveal that men are more likely to be the victims of violent crimes. This means that while men are committing crimes, they are also the ones experiencing it, depending on the category of crime. For example, women are more likely to be victims of domestic violence. More women suffer violence at the hands of men they know than by strangers, and up to two women a week lose their lives as a result.

While men also experience domestic abuse, men face personal and social barriers, as many women do, in reporting domestic abuse, or even telling loved ones about their experiences of it. However, recent ONS (Office for National Statistics) figures suggest that the proportion of men who told police about their

---

2   Public Leaders Network, 'One Woman Dead Every Three Days: Domestic Abuse In Numbers,' *Guardian* (2017) www.theguardian.com/public-leaders-network/2017/dec/14/domestic-abuse-violence-women-femicide-review-refuge-cuts-in-numbers (last accessed 01/12/2018).

3   www.unodc.org/unodc/en/press/releases/2018/November/home--the-most-dangerous-place-for-women--with-majority-of-female-homicide-victims-worldwide-killed-by-partners-or-family--unodc-study-says.html (last accessed 01/12/2018).

domestic abuse increased from 10.4 per cent in 2014–15 to 14.7 per cent in 2018.[4]

Shame is a central, dominant and often debilitating emotion in the male identity. Men are often perceived as less masculine or less of a man for suffering violence at the hands of a woman, and this kind of shaming often comes from other men, the media, and harmful stereotypes within society at large. It's sad to think that society would stigmatise men who experience domestic violence more than they would stigmatise men carrying out violence. Within these discussions, people often focus on heterosexual relationships, erasing LGBTQ+ relationships and experiences of abuse. While men who suffer violence at the hands of a woman may experience shame, men who suffer violence at the hands of another male who may be their partner, may similarly experience shame and trauma.

Needless to say, the overwhelming majority of men are not violent – most women are also not violent. However, men do commit the majority of violent crimes: that needs to be analysed and understood within the context in which it appears. Young boys are often socialised into violence and aggression, to the point that by the time they reach adulthood, they see aggression as the lingua franca of their experiences. Boys are socialised into aggression from a young age, initially through primary socialisation, such as through family and home life. Here, boys build up their identity and self-understanding, and learn what is and isn't acceptable within the household, and in wider society more generally. Children are taught how to form bonds, relationships, how to play and communicate, and, most crucially, how to act – or rather, react. This is largely influenced by what they are exposed to.

---

4   www.ons.gov.uk/peoplepopulationandcommunity/crimeandjustice/bulletins/ domesticabuseinenglandandwales/yearendingmarch2018 (last accessed 28/02/2019).

Like toy soldiers

> There was a conversation that I had recently regarding how
> we who identify as being men, violence is our key commu-
> nicative tool, so inflicting pain on someone else was how I got
> my best friends as a kid . . . – Rhael

The toys that we play with as young boys impact the way we
understand and express ourselves. Boys, in particular, are often
given toys that reflect more aggressive and physical modes of
engagement, such as guns, trucks, hammers and other various
weapons and so forth. A study conducted by Iowa State University
on *The relation of violent and non-violent toys to play behaviour
in pre-schoolers* found that 'Real, pretend, and total aggression
occurred more often in play with violent toys than in play with
nonviolent toys'.[5] That is to say that children generally showed
more aggressive behaviour, whether it was real or pretend, in
play with violent toys than with nonviolent toys.

When I think back on the toys that I grew up playing with,
I recall being given toy guns and action figure heroes, and
consuming content, from cartoons, television shows, music, to
movies, that reinforced and normalised aggressive behaviour
as the norm. Another study, *The Relation Between Toy Gun Play
and Children's Aggressive Behaviour* conducted at Brandeis University,[6] supported the above statement, but also concluded that
parents physically punishing their children resulted in tangible
aggression in both boys and girls, who would revert back to the
violence and aggression that they had been exposed to.

---

5   https://lib.dr.iastate.edu/cgi/viewcontent.cgi?referer=https://www.google.
com/&httpsredir=1&article=11780&context=rtd (last accessed 06/03/2019).
6   www.researchgate.net/publication/234726906_The_Relation_Between_Toy_
Gun_Play_and_Children's_Aggressive_Behavior (last accessed 06/03/2019).

Male violence and aggression is also normalised through secondary socialisation in schools. A culture of toxic masculinity dominates in comprehensive and mixed schools in particular. Among young boys, play fighting is often a sign of friendship. Two boys who are not friends generally do not play fight with each other. However, play fighting can and often does lead to real fighting – when one feels the other has gone too far, or they feel embarrassed or humiliated, particularly in front of their peers. From a young age, we exercise aggression as a means of socialising and entering manhood. We can understand male aggression as hierarchy: a way of testing who is the strongest among the group, without actually getting into a fight. This helps to establish the social hierarchy of the male group – which is often based on physical characteristics associated with maleness, such as strength, rather than kindness or empathy (which is typically associated with femininity). Often it feels like a holding rank, where you are treated with respect if you are deemed strong, and with much less respect if you show public displays of weakness. Once you get into a physical fight, everything changes, and your position in that hierarchy can dramatically shift at any moment. Think of the classic Peter Parker/Spiderman scenario, where the social pariah or 'nerd', who is considered to be weak, beats up the jock who is supposedly the strongest, suddenly gaining 'street credibility' and popularity, moving up the ladder.

Male aggression is also a performance. At a younger age, men feel pressure, often from other men, to express desirability to the girls within their school setting who they may be attracted to and have not yet developed the language to express it. Physical play fighting helps the boy to stand out in front of the girl(s), while also maintaining, or even accumulating, rank and respect among the boys.

One of the most profoundly bizarre aspects of masculinity, or when men identify within the remit of masculinity, is there is a severe lack of intimacy (non-sexual) with their own gender.
– Jordan S

We also play fight as young boys in order to fulfil the absence of an intimate touch that we no longer experience; the touch that we were used to during pre-adolescence. 'Intimate' here does not mean romantic, but relates to being cared for. As we grow into our adolescence, boys are generally socialised into and expected to be strong, stoic, physical, to stand alone, to be a real 'man', so the soft and intimate touch that we may have been used to during our childhood disappears. Play fighting is a way of re-establishing that, but within the confines of acceptable patriarchal masculinity: boys won't be ostracised for engaging in physical interaction when it's violent or aggressive.

Often, the violence that plays out between men as adults has seeds in these seemingly playful acts of aggression, where men live up to the expectations that have been placed on their manhood for the longest time. The aggression towards women that many men feel later on in life has been linked to lack of conversation and education which eventually leads to the inability to process emotions and feelings of anger and rage. There is also the issue of internal anger and repressed rage that a lot of young boys grow up with and grown men still have, which has a significant impact on their mental health.

Depression, alienation and suicide

During a period in my early twenties, I felt alone, isolated, withdrawn, and lethargic. I could not understand why I felt the way I was feeling; how everything, every effort, felt futile and meaningless. It felt as though I required twice as much effort to do half the task. Each day felt more and more tiring, like I was on a long journey to somewhere without a destination and was running out of fuel. I did not have someone to talk to about this feeling, and I did not know how to talk anyone, so I tried to hide it as best I could; by always uplifting other people, by being positive towards others, being funny, being upbeat, being happy, all of which were surface level expressions. Deep down I was in agonising torment; I was experiencing profound pain beyond the physical level. To me, it was clear I was going through a lot, so I thought everyone around me could see it. I felt exposed, as though the pain showed on my skin. I was shocked to discover that no else noticed it; no one noticed how I had changed, how something in me was dying. When no one came forward to offer their support; a shoulder to cry on, a safe space, someone to talk to, when no one heard my muted cry for help, I felt I had to go through it alone. I isolated myself further because I believed that I was the only person who could help me with the way that I was feeling.

There are so many boys and men who feel like this: who feel they have to suffer alone and have no one to talk to, no outlet, no release. Some do go through it and come out better, but for many, the repression eats at them with fatal consequences. The statistics on men suffering from various mental health issues are quite shocking and should be cause for national, if not international, concern. Here are some statistics from Men's Health Forum, 2017:[7]

- Approximately three out of every four suicides (76 per cent) are by men

---

7   www.menshealthforum.org.uk/key-data-mental-health (last accessed 06/03/2019).

- Suicide is the biggest killer of men under the age of 35
- 12.5 per cent of men (over one in ten) are suffering from one of the common mental health disorders (e.g. anxiety and panic disorders, depression, bipolar disorder, substance abuse and addiction)
- The rate of depression in men is estimated to be at 8 per cent (12 per cent for women). However, men are also less likely to seek professional help or access mental health services. It is also reported that men have significantly lower access to social support via friends, relatives and local community

Further statistics, this time relating specifically to young people and young adults, from Young Minds, the UK's leading charity for children and young people's mental health, include:[8]

- One in five young adults have a diagnosable mental health disorder (one in ten among children)
- One in twelve young people have or will self-harm at some point in their lives
- One in three adult mental health conditions relate directly to adverse or traumatic childhood experiences

Here are some additional interesting figures – though not specifically statistics on mental health, they paint a picture of factors that may contribute to mental health problems and depict the reality of life for many men in modern society:[9]

---

8   https://youngminds.org.uk/about-us/media-centre/mental-health-stats/?gclid=CjoKCQjw45_bBRD_ARIsAJ6wUXQgduRWox4PfY-Oa7U2HTxlCJjDR9c-FKnn8VIpKokqy-gPMGTZnJgaAjfbEALw_wcB (last accessed 01/12/2018).
9   www.menshealthforum.org.uk/key-data-mental-health (last accessed 05/03/2019).

- 87 per cent of homeless people/rough sleepers are men
- Men are three times more likely to become alcohol dependent, and three times as likely to report frequent drug use (than women)
- Men make up 95 per cent of the prison population

I think that men on average are more prone to extreme or more violent forms of behaviour, and suicide is a form of violent behaviour. – Matt

In an article in *The British Psychological Society*, Swani, Payne and Stanistreet examine a relationship they argue has largely been taking for granted: the relationship between aggression and suicide. They argue that women are attempting suicide at a high rate, but that

an important difference in completed suicide between women and men relates to their method of choice. Men are more likely to die by suicide using violent methods with higher lethality, such as by using firearms, or hanging . . . because such methods are congruent with dominant constructions of masculinity that prescribe aggression and strength.[10]

This suggests that the aggression that men are socialised into is not only something that can lead to mental health problems, but can also be what stops them surviving suicide attempts when compared to women. This is where we see how aggression, violence and mental health are interrelated.

---

10 https://thepsychologist.bps.org.uk/volume-21/edition-4/masculinities-and-suicide (last accessed 15/03/2019).

When we talk about patriarchal society, we must focus on the ways in which women are oppressed as a result of the system. However, the notion that men benefit from the system, in all aspects of their lives, is misguided. It is clear that men are suffering, almost to the point of a national epidemic: toxic masculinity thrives on a vicious cycle where men contribute to it and also suffer from it. While we cannot dismantle oppressive structures overnight, there should be strategies and interventions in place to help men – as well as women – cope better with mental health issues. The media and popular culture play a powerful role in society, and they often dictate that men should not talk about their feelings, that men should suffer emotionally and mentally in silence. As long as there is taboo around mental health, serious issues, such as suicide, will continue to be overlooked and swept under the carpet.

When guys are going through great periods of stress and experiencing things that are holding them back and causing them pain, they'll keep it to themselves and not tell their partners. There are cases of men who have died by suicide, and there are cases where their spouses or children just didn't know anything. And then they'll learn afterwards that they didn't want to be a burden to their family around them. – Jordan H

Mental health and austerity

All statistics on mental health have to be considered within the context of our current society and political climate. In *The Violence of Austerity*, Mary O'Hara claims that 'Mental health services in the UK, are notoriously underfunded and often referred to as a "Cinderella" service'. She points to statistics from the Centre for Economic Performance, which reveal that mental health services receive 13 per cent of the total NHS budget, while mental illness is responsible for 23 per cent of the loss of years of healthy life caused by all illnesses worldwide.[11] O'Hara also points to the factors of social welfare in contributing to mental health issues, revealing how society can be both the cause of our poor health, and also limit our chances of getting treatment, through underfunding and cuts to public services.

Ongoing cuts to public services also mean that resources have been slashed when it comes to community centres and youth centres. In the *London's Lost Youth Services 2018* report, Green Party member, Sian Berry, reported that from 2011–18, there had been a 44 per cent youth service budget cut, with the average council taking £1.5 million out of youth services over this time.[12] Lack of community centres is notoriously linked to an uptick in violent crime. Aggression, violence and mental health issues are not just the responsibilities of individuals, but it is society's responsibility to try to help rehabilitate young men.

Mental health in the public eye

Male mental health is a growing conversation, which, in recent years, has received much needed attention from organisations and institutions, as well as the media and high profile figures and celebrities. Grime artist/MC/entrepreneur Stormzy, who's debut album *Gang Signs & Prayer* reached number 1 in the UK charts, broke down taboo around mental health, particularly in younger circles. The album itself touches on many essential issues including mental health, anxiety and depression. In the first verse of the opening song *First Things First*, he says 'you was

---

11 Vickie Cooper and David Whyte, *The Violence of Austerity* (Pluto Press, 2017), 37.
12 www.london.gov.uk/sites/default/files/2018_03_20_sb_londons_lost_youth_services_2018_final.pdf (last accessed 19/03/2019).

fighting with your girl/and I was fighting my depression.' I was struck by these lyrics, in particular, by the word 'depression'. I had listened to Stormzy and witnessed his meteoric rise within the music industry, but did not expect any part of his music to touch on mental health, although it was so important that it did. Following this, Stormzy went on to speak to *Channel 4 News*, the *Guardian* and on *The Jonathan Ross Show*, sharing his experience of depression and saying,

> I feel like it's important and needs to be spoken about . . . I know it sounds so cliched but genuinely, I thought there will be young kids who look at me and probably have the same thing that I think about so many other people: 'I bet you they never felt like this.'

Other high profile male voices have spoken out about mental health in recent years, including rapper and actor Professor Green, who spoke about his struggles on his documentary *Suicide and Me*. Actor Dwayne 'The Rock' Johnson has also spoken out about his struggles with depression, while best-selling author Matt Haig, most notably through his books *Reasons To Stay Alive* and *Notes on a Nervous Planet,* has shared his experiences of mental health issues, in particular anxiety and depression.

When Chester Bennington, lead singer of the US rock band LINKIN PARK died by suicide in July 2017, there was outcry across the US media and internationally: it came as a shock. Chester had, in recent interviews, spoken about his struggles with mental health and suicidal thoughts. He had also written about such sensitive subjects through LINKIN PARK's music. It was this music that I also really related to as a teenager, and as an adult, and would listen to so that I can get through my darkest days, hoping I was not alone. When news of Chester's suicide spread, I saw many of my male friends also post dedications to him and how his band's music had helped them. It was then that I realised that so many of us were going through the same thing as young boys transitioning to manhood, and we all thought we were going through it alone.

As well as Chester Bennington's death, other high profile male suicides in recent years include world famous American actor Robin Williams, TV personality, chef and author Anthony Bourdain, South Korean singer and songwriter Kim Jonghyun, British fashion designer Alexander McQueen, Welsh former professional football player and manager Gary Speed, American television show host and producer Don Cornelius, and American actor Lee Thompson Young, to name but a few. These men were various ages, came from various cultural backgrounds, had various ethnicities and were not all suffering from the exact same mental health issue. They were also men who were considered to be successful; the idea that success automatically prevents you from suffering from depression is a misguided notion that causes people to stigmatise mental health issues as something people can snap out of if their life is seemingly 'good', while it can cause people to internalise that stigma, and further deny their own illness. Mental health issues can affect all sorts of people and communities, across the spectrum.

I would always ask all of my male friends how are you? Really casually. And they'll say I'm fine. And then I'll ask them again . . . and then on the third how have you been? I have to prepare myself for an hour of their response . . . I say to all my friends, just ask a guy how he is three times, and on the third time, you normally get (an answer). Because how are you can seem a really flippant question . . . I don't think it's our responsibility, I think women have got enough on our plates. But I do feel like it is something that in a human way, it's definitely a contribution that is worth doing. – Julie

Men do not always have the emotional language to discuss their feelings or experiences, even with friends, family or loved ones, and so we often benefit from high profile voices, particularly men, speaking out about their mental health struggles. Hearing from others can really help to open up the conversation by watching an illness which has a long history of taboo attached to it become normalised and humanised before your own eyes. Typically, notions of manhood and masculinity reinforce the idea that men do not, or should not, suffer from mental health issues such as anxiety or depression because it makes them weak. And so, high-profile men and public figures help people to understand that many of us go through the same thing, bridging the gap between mental health and the male identity. However, even they face backlash and are sometimes told to 'man up'. For example, in 2017, journalist and TV presenter Piers Morgan tweeted in response to new statistics, '34 million UK adults are mentally ill? Man up, Britain, and focus on those who REALLY need help.' Often, it is difficult to open up and speak to the people around you, so when a celebrity or even a stranger, says that they are going through what you are going through; anxiety, depression, hopelessness, it validates your feelings. It makes you feel like you are normal for going through it because someone you admire is also going through it; it also gives you hope when the person has gone through it already and come out the other side – it makes you feel like you can too. But damaging comments from celebrities such as those telling people to 'man up', can also stop people from getting the help they need. Widespread concern about mental health issues when a shocking story is released in the press about a high-profile figure is a positive, but the same level of attention, empathy and care should be extended to all individuals who are suffering, beyond the public realm.

There are a number of reasons why a person may decide to take their own life; it is often ambiguous and unclear to others, and sometimes unclear to the person suffering. For many men, it may stem from issues of internalised rage and anger resulting from existing trauma, such as abuse, or feelings of utter hopelessness and an inability (or a lack of desire) to cope with life – depression. Nonetheless, it's essential to ensure that people feel supported before mental health issues reach a crisis stage. Charities such as Young Minds fight for preventative strategies at earlier stages in young people's lives, where they are particularly vulnerable to suffering from mental health issues.

The stigma around men, masculinity and mental health will only begin to change once the shaming and silencing of men who suffer from it ends. We need to have more men who are open and expressive about their experiences and struggles with mental health, but also their everyday experiences, not just the struggles. The more men and boys are allowed to express themselves, especially in an emotional way, without judgement (from other men, in particular), the sooner we will see a positive change. This needs to happen from boyhood. In the documentary on boyhood and masculinity, *The Mask You Live In*, Dr. Niobe Way claims 'at the exact age we begin to hear emotional language disappear in boys narrative in the national data, that's exactly the age boys begin to have suicide rates higher by five times than girls'.

Writing poetry and keeping a diary helped me so much with my own mental health struggles, expressing myself and understanding my thoughts. Where I thought I had no one to talk to, or did not feel comfortable speaking to anyone else – largely due to the fact that I was concerned about being judged or not being understood – I would write in my diary. I would express myself through writing, and that kind of expression, although not an absolute solution, did help alleviate some of the burdens I faced at the time. A lot of men need this open, expressive medium as well as communal support. We need to stop treating mental health and all the illnesses that fall under it such as depression and suicide as isolated incidents and come together to support one another, free of judgement, in spaces that are safe, loving and transformative. Above all, we need to challenge the cuts being made to health services, fighting for everyone to have adequate access to treatment, which can be lifesaving.

Chapter 3

What's love got to do with it?: Love, sex and consent

If emotions are so weak, why are we the ones running away from them. – Rhael

I was raised on love songs; RnB, Slow Jams, Soul, Pop, Congolese rhumba, music of the early 2000s where topics such as love, longing and heartache were the norm; listening to artists and bands such as Jagged Edge, Joe, Boys II Men, Backstreet Boys, N-Sync, Eternal, Destiny's Child, En Vogue, Marvin Gaye, Okay Jazz, Papa Wemba, Shola Ama, Craig David, Another Level, Daniel Bedingfield and Maxwell. I would listen to songs such as Boys II Men's 'End of the Road' and sing along as if I was the one going through the break up. Or 'Let's Get Married' by Jagged Edge, imagining the day that I too would walk down the aisle. The culture of romantic love was virtually inescapable.

When I was in primary school, I had a huge crush on a classmate that I was also neighbours with; she lived in the same block on our estate but our flat was a floor or two above hers. One spring morning, I decided to write a letter expressing my affection for her. To get the letter to her, I folded it into a paper aeroplane and threw it so it glided gently to her balcony. The letter glided past, landing in the communal back garden of the estate. So I wrote another. I kept re-writing, throwing and missing, until finally, around the tenth try, the love letter paper aeroplane landed on her balcony. A few hours later, as she went to walk her dog, I waited in anticipation to see how she would react to finding the letters. I later discovered that the estate caretaker had got to the letters and disposed of them before they could be found. I spent many evenings gazing into her balcony, wondering if she knew. Trying to find the courage to proclaim my love to her but I never did.

Looking back, I realised that all the love songs I grew up listening to as a young boy had encouraged and nurtured an emotional empathy and openness in expression, which would later be radically discouraged during my adolescent and teenage years. I was an emotionally expressive boy, and many of the boys in my primary school were too. But by the time I had reached secondary school, I was claiming that love was something I wasn't interested in, that I had no emotions, that it was for boys who were soft – somewhere along the line I had transitioned into a man with a hard exterior, as did many of the boys I grew up with. There are different shades to the male experience as we will explore later, but from a straight male perspective, it felt like men were being socialised out of love, while women were socialised into love.

Men are often socialised out of love, in the sense that emotional empathy is no longer the norm, or even a desirable trait, while emotional detachment is something to aspire to. Women tend to be socialised into love, or an idea of love – often as a way to reinforce traditional gender roles. From a young age, women are prepared, often by their families or by wider society, to be someone's wife: they are domesticated, taught or expected to cook and clean, which is often less to do with self-sufficiency, but more to do with preparing to be a 'good wife' to a hypothetical future husband. So much so that you can often have a boy and a girl who grew up in the same household, and by the time both become independent, the girl is performing household duties, while the boy barely has a grasp on it. As well as carrying the burden of this physical labour, the pressure placed on women to care for men, sacrifice their own ambitions, or submit to make a man feel stronger or more intelligent, requires 'emotional' labour.

Players only

Men are afforded certain privileges within the dynamics of love, relationships and sex in particular. The same kind of sexual behaviour that a woman is ostracised for is not only deemed acceptable, but praise-worthy for a man. Consider men who have been exposed as unfaithful in the public eye: they are forgiven by society much more easily, whereas women are branded with a scarlet letter. The myth that men have a higher sex drive is often used to explain men's behaviour, while women who are unfaithful often have their lives tarnished, the label sticking with them for a long time, often without forgiveness. Single men with multiple partners are labelled as *player, pimp, Casanova, womaniser, heartbreaker*. Yet women are labelled with *whore, slut, hoe, j-bag, jezebel, tart, slapper, slut, prozzy (prostitute)*, The list is never-ending, and seems to update itself every year with new words.

Women have attempted to reclaim these labels – for example, Amber Rose created 'Slut Walk' in 2011; a movement calling for an end to rape culture, victim blaming and slut-shaming. Misogynistic labelling exists to disempower and shame women, taking away their right to be free sexual beings, while men are given more and more control over sex: *'everything in the world is about sex except sex, sex is about power'*. Ultimately, labelling of any sort to stigmatise people for engaging in consensual sex is more often than not another way for men to reinforce oppressive gender dynamics.

Sex as initiation into manhood

I don't want a ritual into manhood, because that's not something that I conceive for myself. – Tom

Expectations around sex vary for men and women. Men and women are pressured into sex, but in different ways. From an early age, many boys are pressured to think about sex, to want to have sex, and to have sex as early as possible. Often, it is other boys or men who put that pressure onto boys, where sex becomes a rite of passage into manhood, and it's almost inconceivable for a boy not to have had sex by the time they have reached a particular age. Girls are often expected to remain 'pure' and remain virgins for as long as possible, sometimes until marriage – although this view depends on cultural norms and expectations.

The pressure placed on young boys to have sex can lead to the erasure of cases where young boys have had sex under the age of consent. When a boy below the consenting age has sex with an older girl or woman, we often fail to acknowledge it as a case of rape or sexual abuse. Preconceived notions of masculinity tell us that boys cannot be taken advantage of sexually by older women. The younger the boy is, the more accomplished, the more 'manly' he is should he have sex with an older girl or woman. The praise often comes from older men. In an interview with the *Daily Mail* in 2013,[1] American singer, songwriter and actor,

---

1 'Far Too Young! Chris Brown reveals he was just eight years old when he lost his virginity as he compares himself to Prince,' *Daily Mail* (5 October 2013) www. dailymail.co.uk/tvshowbiz/article-2445396/Chris-Brown-reveals-8-lost-virginity-compares-Prince.html (last accessed 25/04/2019).

Chris Brown, reveals he was just eight years old when he lost his virginity as he compares himself to Prince.[2] Brown revealed that he 'lost his virginity' at only eight years old, with a girl who was around fourteen or fifteen years old. He claimed that by that age, he was already watching pornography. It is worth noting the media's language around this. All of the outlets report that eight was the age at which he lost his virginity: no mention of the fact that he was raped, sexually abused or even taken advantage of. An eight-year-old girl having sex with a fourteen or fifteen-year-old-boy is statutory rape – but notice how the reaction and language is different when it comes to the eight-year-old boy. This shows how boys are conditioned into thinking that sex is something to be celebrated when they are involved, rather than challenged.

Chris Brown claimed: 'At eight, being able to do it, kind of preps you for the long run, so you can be a beast at it . . . most women won't have any complaints if they've been with me. They can't really complain. It's all good.' This quote reveals a lot, particularly, how at the tender age of eight years old, Brown was already exposed to sex and the idea that a man must please women. It also shows just how much a man's identity and worth tends to be tied to how well they perform sex; that sex is the apogee of their interactions with women, and that is what firmly roots them as a man.

Pornography as reality

There are a lot of people who learn to have sex directly through porn. – Julie

This perception of sex as a mandatory initiation into manhood has existed for centuries, but has been exacerbated with

2 Ibid.

technology, and the increasing ease with which sexual content can be consumed. More men than ever are watching pornography, while more boys are being exposed to pornography at a younger age, which is leading to sexual addictions, problems with intimacy, a desire for isolation and damaging relationships. Many young people are left to learn about sex and sex education through pornography, which seems to be where the issue stems from.

Reports suggest that 90 per cent of boys are exposed to pornography by the age of 18, with the average age of exposure being only 11 years old, and that men are more likely to look at porn than women (this isn't to suggest that women do not watch pornography, as it is reported that one in three porn viewers are women).[3] In London, the One Harley Street clinic has seen a 100 per cent rise in referrals for porn addiction in the last six years.[4] Former NFL Professional Athlete and Actor, star of hit TV shows *Everybody Hates Chris* and *Brooklyn 99*, Terry Crews said in 2014 in a Facebook live stream viewed by over 3 million people, how porn had 'messed up his life'. He went on to say:

> Some people say, 'hey man, you can't really be addicted to pornography.' But I'm gonna tell you something: if day turns to night and you are still watching, you probably have got a problem. And that was me . . . It (pornography) changes the way you think about people. People become objects. People become body parts; they become things to be used rather than people to be loved.

---

3   www.huffingtonpost.com/elwood-d-watson/pornography-addiction-amo_b_5963460.html (last accessed 01/12/2018).
4   www.standard.co.uk/news/health/number-of-londoners-seeking-help-for-porn-addiction-soars-a3841541.html (last accessed 05/03/2019).

Much of the pornographic content produced by the industry is largely centred around male sexual fantasy and gratification, which often relies on misogynistic or racist tropes. Pornography is not a true reflection of the kind of sex that the average person has; nor is it a reflection of the kind of body the average person has. Furthermore, over the years, pornography has become increasingly violent and misogynistic. One of the effects of this is the way that men speak about and refer to sex. The colloquial language men use to describe sex reflects this exacerbation of violence and misogyny in pornography. Here are some examples of the different ways having sex is generally referred to by men; *beat, smash, crush, press, pump, bang, screw, pound, hit,* just to name a few – you'll notice how violent the language is. The use of this language in order to refer to sex removes the intimacy of sex, and dehumanises the personal aspect of it, reducing sex to a mere action, physical and aggressive at its most reductive, and framed as something a man does to a woman, rather than a mutual engagement, and something the woman also enjoys.

Virginity and Incels

In 2014, a 22-year-old man named Elliot Rodgers, from Santa Barbara, California committed a mass shooting, murdering six people and injuring fourteen. He left behind a series of videos and a 'manifesto' uploaded to YouTube, titled 'Rodgers Retribution'. In this video, Rogers vouched his hatred for women. This hatred stemmed from his rejection by women that were sexually active with other men. He also expressed profound resentment and bitterness over his status of virginity, and ultimately characterised the deadly shooting yet to come as punishment for the above. Soon after the news broke, Rodgers was identified by media outlets, social media and the online world as a part of

Incel culture, based largely on his own videos. He was labelled a hero by some, and a monster by others. Incels self-define as 'involuntary celibates', and incel culture is largely an online subculture that has been growing in intensity in recent years. While it paints a terrifying picture, the picture fits perfectly within modern-day toxic masculinity.

Incels believe they have specific rights when it comes to being a man and being sexually active: rights which stand in stark contrast to those they grant to women. They believe in the redistribution of sex, which works on the assumption that men are owed and entitled to sex from women, and should be able to receive it on demand. Our initial reaction may be to argue that no human being truly believes they are entitled to another human being's body. But misogyny and rape culture thrive off the idea that men are entitled to women's bodies: an idea that has been reinforced by the patriarchy throughout history, for as long as we can remember. Today, rape culture takes a different shape and form, hidden in pop song lyrics, its messages shrouded in 'comedy' in TV programmes, but the age-old and damaging belief is still there. Media headlines use dehumanising language when it comes to the women they are discussing and we wonder why people are uneducated when it comes to misogyny and rape culture. The little education people may receive about it through conversations with women, parents or teachers, is often undone by the normalisation of toxic masculinity in the mainstream. The media, liberal Hollywood and the music industry will of course express outrage at an incident like the Rodgers shooting, but they are much slower to condemn the role that popular culture, which may include their films, TV programmes and songs, contributes to it.

The fact that Incels are moving from the online sphere to real life is reflective of our modern-day dangerous era, where we currently run the risk of increasingly misogynistic violence against women with fatal consequences. The media character-ised Rodgers' attack as spurred on by mental health issues (in Chapter 5, I discuss the issues with media characterisations of 'lone wolf' political acts of violence). Although many would not dispute that Rodgers was suffering from mental health issues of some sort, the fact remains that there is not a similar record of women with mental health issues carrying out mass acts of violence against men. We discussed myths of masculinity and the 'men are trash trope' in Chapter 1. Women using a phrase like this has caused public outcry to the point where men argue that their masculinity is 'in crisis' and needs to be protected. But women speaking out against misogynistic societal ideals have not resulted in the mass murder of men by women. It is by no means an equal playing field, as some men would suggest. The more that misogynistic violence is put down to an individual 'lone wolf' mentality rather than identified as caused by widespread harmful ideologies, the less chance we have of overcoming it. Elliot Rodgers' attack was abhorrent, but this is where we see that rape culture, misogyny and patriarchy do cause some men to lose out in the end – Rodgers died by suicide at the scene of the attack.

Rape culture and consent

Rape culture is not about every single man going out and committing a terrible sexual assault, it's about how men in this world are complicit in allowing other men to commit these crimes. – Elrick

The presence of Incels raises questions about rape culture: misguided notions of consent play a vital role in this. After the

47

#MeToo movement, many have argued that consent is a conversation that needs to start from a young age: in my view, it should be taught as part of sex education. Consent is defined in the Oxford Dictionary as *permission for something to happen, or agreement to do something*. With regards to sex, it means actively agreeing to sexual activity with someone. It is important to emphasise that consent is the presence of a yes; not the absence of a no, meaning just because someone does not say no, does not mean that they said yes. There are many ways in which people can freeze and do not say 'no' out loud. Psychologist James Hopper claims 'In the midst of sexual assault, the brain's fear circuitry dominates . . . *freezing* is a brain-based response to detecting danger. Think deer in headlights.[5] Many victims of sexual assault have come forward and described this response. The issue of consent extends beyond rape to interactions, for instance, inappropriate touching or catcalling: the consent of women is compromised on a daily basis through male abuse of power.

A patriarchal society teaches men two particular things about sex with a woman:

1. Sex is transactional – that sex can (and supposedly rightfully) be acquired through purchase. For example, think of a scenario where a man believes that paying for a date should lead to sex. Or that any kind of material/ financial expense spent on a woman – or even just being nice – should be rewarded with sex. Of course, overwhelmingly, men do not behave in this way on absolute terms – however, this thinking still prevails. Many men do

---

5   www.washingtonpost.com/news/grade-point/wp/2015/06/23/why-many-rape-victims-dont-fight-or-yell/?noredirect=on&utm_term=.fabcc159d50e (last accessed 20/03/2019).

not think in these terms, but those that do may not spot the connection.

2. That sex is negotiable – that sex can be negotiated. That 'no' doesn't mean 'no'. Rather, it means that you need to work harder to get them to say yes. This thinking in particular is played out in TV shows, romantic comedies and other mainstream media; that the man who is persistent eventually wins the woman (rather than just being the man who has worn her down and compromised her consent or autonomy – which sounds far less romantic and ideal).

It's important to emphasise that it's not simply about whether or not a man gets to have sex: rather, it is about the power dynamic within which sex occurs. For example, sex work is a scenario where men usually pay women for sex. Transaction, in this instance, differs to conceiving of sex as transactional when paying for a date. While there are issues with sex work being unsafe for women – a big factor in this is the criminalisation of sex work which creates unsafe working conditions – it is a form of work for many women, usually working-class women, around the world. Many men oppose going to sex workers on the grounds that it compromises their masculinity to have to pay a woman for sex. Yet, men are happy to *expect* sex after paying for a date – many men don't want to outwardly pay for sex, wanting it to appear as though the woman was attracted to them without them having to do so, yet they expect sex if they 'fork out' money on a woman. The idea that sex can be negotiated is reflected in statistics on industries with the highest reported levels of sexual assault. Women who are vulnerable, marginalised or in precarious work situations without adequate representation, experience disproportionate abuse: the healthcare and social assistance industry accounts for 11.5 per cent of sexual harassment claims, in large part, because the sector is dominated by women, and particularly, women of colour.[6]

Consent is difficult for many men to grasp because it calls into question an automatic sense of entitlement, where men don't feel they need to look out for the signs. Being given the go ahead from women does not always cross their minds in a society where men are told that women's bodies are accessible for them – that in many ways, women's bodies function *for* men's entertainment. But many men appear to understand the significance of consent when asked about it in relation to the women in their lives; mothers, sisters, daughters, etc. Some men become strong advocates for gender equality and the treatment of women when they become fathers to a girl (at least for their own daughter) – fathers often warn their daughters to look out for and be careful around predatory men, and men in general. They feel a sense of duty towards her; where previously, this empathy would have been conditioned or socialised out of them – but it's usually from the relational position of possession. Men are acutely aware of the behaviours of other men, even men that they know, when it comes to sex and the imbalance of power in relationships.

Where consent is not given, it is unequivocally rape. But rape itself is often debated, even when no consent has been given. The following statements are examples of what is often said by people: *what were you wearing? were you drunk? did you lead him on? were you in a relationship with him?* This shifts responsibility from the perpetrator to the victim; i.e. victim blaming. Do we ask these questions when other crimes are committed? e.g. when someone is robbed of their possessions, they are asked *are you okay?* or *what time did it happen?*, not *what were you wearing?*

---

6   www.vox.com/identities/2017/11/21/16685942/sexual-harassment-industry-service-retail (last accessed 04/04/2019).

or *have you had too much to drink?* Furthermore, suggesting that rape can be avoided through safety measures such as not dressing 'provocatively', or being out late alone or being drunk, reinforces the idea that men are predators by default; as if rape is something that is a part of men's genetic makeup which means that they can't be helped if the circumstances suit them. Again, this reinforces victim blaming, putting the onus on women to not become victims: as though this is an inevitable fate for them.

The statistics on rape in the UK are quite frightening. Rape Crisis England & Wales reports the following:

- Approximately 85,000 women and 12,000 men are raped in England and Wales every year. That equates to 11 rapes per hour
- 1 in 5 women aged 16–59 has experienced some form of sexual violence since the age of 16
- Approximately 90 per cent of those who are raped knew the perpetrator prior to the offence
- Roughly 15 per cent of those who experience sexual violence choose to report to the police (only 1 rape in every 14 reported to police ends up with a conviction)

Rape is an issue that affects women all around the world and affects women of all ages. There is also the very serious issue of male victims of rape. Often, this is overlooked, as men who are raped are shamed and embarrassed because it compromises their masculinity; it is seen as though they are less of a man, or weak, or bizarre for refusing sex or being overpowered, so there are many cases of men not reporting the crime; men have also reported incidents of arriving at the police station and not being taken seriously.

In a 2018 storyline of the British soap opera *Coronation Street*, one of the principal characters of the show David Platt, played by actor Jack Shepherd, was raped by his personal trainer Josh Tucker, played by actor, and former professional rugby player, Ryan Clayton, after a night out. The storyline followed David's journey and experience of shame of being raped (by a man), fear (of also contracting HIV), embarrassment and anger, as well as some of the complications of pursuing a charge with the authorities and the difficulties of confronting the rapist. It was an eye-opening story, which caused a lot of uproar and discussion, as this issue is so rarely spoken about, let alone represented on national television. The actor Ryan Clayton, as reported by The Sun newspaper, had this to say: 'It's really well written and the way they've worked with Survivors Manchester as well, they worked very closely. They're making it as realistic as possible.'[7] The fact that the show worked with real life male rape survivors makes it very powerful, as it is not just about creating a controversial or sensational storyline, which is a road the show could have gone down, but about representing the everyday lived experience of real people. Half a century ago, male rape wasn't even considered to be real – something we discuss in Chapter 6 – let alone represented on a national soap opera.

Ultimately, rape continues to exist, at this rate, largely because we live in a society that normalises *rape culture*; that is to say, it trivialises sexual abuse. If the epidemic of rape is to end, young people need to be taught about consent as part of their sex education, and support must be provided, as opposed to the shaming that takes place when incidents do arise.

---

7 Carl Greenwood, 'Coronation Street's Ryan Clayton Defends Dark Rape Storyline As Josh Tucker Sexually Assaults David Platt,' *Sun* (2018). www.thesun.co.uk/tvandshowbiz/5831988/coronation-streets-ryan-clayton-defends-dark-rape-storyline-as-josh-tucker-sexually-assaults-david-platt (last accessed 05/12/2018).

Chapter 4

This is a man's world: The politics of masculinity, the masculinity of politics

Here's the beginning of a bad joke; what do Benito Mussolini (former Prime Minister of Italy, 1922–43), General Augusto Pinochet (former President of Chile, 1974–90), Mobutu Sese Seko (former President of DR Congo, 1965–97) all have in common? Is it bad hairlines? Badly designed hats? Fashion sense that was slightly out of touch? It's hard to tell. What about if I add some more names to that list, Idi Amin (former President of Uganda, 1971–9), General Francisco Franco (former President of Spain, 1939–75), Kim Jong-Il (former Supreme Leader of North Korea, 1994–2011), does it become a little clearer? The answer is: they were dictators, and they were all men. In fact, the vast majority of dictators in the modern era, and further back in history, have been men.

My family fled President Mobutu's dictatorial regime in the DR Congo, then Zaire, and resettled in the United Kingdom as refugees in the early 1990s. This dictatorship had been a huge topic of conversation in our household and our Congolese community growing up, detailing the experiences; some mild, others harrowing. My parents told us about tanks rolling through the city, soldiers shooting at civilians, student activist friends being thrown indefinitely in jail or going missing, but also about the mandatory songs that were sung in praise of Mobutu, about god-like portrayals of a so-called omnipotent ruler, and the extraordinary mythological stories this entailed; how he fought off and killed a leopard with his bare hands, and re-named himself Mobutu Sese Seko Nkuku Ngbendu Wa Za Banga meaning 'The all-powerful warrior who, because of his endurance and inflexible will to win, goes from conquest to conquest leaving fire in his wake.'

I used to wonder what would make a man want to have all that power at once or to be worshipped like this? Ego? Greed? Control? None of those appeared to exclusively answer the question, but they all contributed to the wider picture. As I got older, I started reflecting more on how boys are socialised into domination and violence – fighting, playing with toy guns and toy soldiers as part of imaginary war games. Patriarchal society normalises male dominance.

It is of little surprise, then, that the overwhelming majority of dictators have been men. More generally, heads of state and world leaders have been men, throughout history through to the present day. Figures from a United Nations report states that only 22 per cent of all national parliamentarians are women, which is a small increase from 11 per cent in 1995.[1] From October 2017, only eleven women were serving as Head of State and twelve as Head of Government. It is worth noting that there are 195 countries in the world, and that women make up 49.6 per cent of the world's population.

Fighting, conflict, and war are, to a certain degree, idealised in the modern day, for example, through popular video games

---

[1] www.unwomen.org/en/what-we-do/leadership-and-political-participation/facts-and-figures (last accessed 05/12/2018).

such as *Call of Duty*, *God of War* and *Halo*. The effect of these games is not only that extreme violence is normalised, and a social talking point for boys and men, but these games also constantly reinforce the idea of an 'Other'; an enemy. Many boys grow up thinking that there is always someone to fight against, inculcating a kill or be killed mentality: another element of toxic masculinity. The pressures usually start from a young age and carry on through to adulthood, translating from the virtual world to the real world.

I can recall, hanging out on the housing estate I grew up in as a young boy, with a group of friends: one of the boys said my friend (let's call him James) had claimed he could beat me up. Unbeknownst to me at the time, some of our other friends were telling James that it was me who had said I could beat him. I was confused because I thought we were friends: why would James want to fight me? By the time we saw each other, the negative way I had been socialised into dealing with situations, through violence rather than talking, had kicked in. James and I got into a fight, with the rest of the crowd of boys watching, cheering, jeering until we were eventually separated. I was very reluctant to get into a fight – I knew it was wrong as soon as it had begun, but I did not want to be the person who was beaten, the person who was weaker. I had been taught that violence was a natural part of handling things. After the fight, I apologised immediately to James – there wasn't much damage done to either of us; we were both scrawny, skinny kids who barely knew how to swing a punch, let alone actually do any damage – and we made up.

The majority of children who are socialised into violence through fighting or video games aren't all of a sudden leading a call to arms or declaring international war, however, the way that society normalises violence against an 'enemy' impacts the way that we as a society justify acts of war or military conquests and invasions through the construction of an 'other' that we need to dominate or supposedly protect ourselves against. Consider the 2003 invasion of Iraq, which led to the Iraq war, where Saddam Hussein was accused of hiding 'weapons of mass destruction' – he quickly became an enemy of the West, with the UK joining forces with the US to thwart his so-called plans to use them. Or the more recent military invasion of Libya. Think of the way Muslims, ethnic minorities and refugees are constantly posited as threats to western society, leading to white male groups such as the Alt-right arguing that they are protecting their own 'kind'. In fact, men are so heavily socialised into war and conflict as resolution, you hardly ever see non-violent solutions or courses of action taken as the more superior form of conflict resolution. Rather, the rhetoric from male political leaders often makes light of the violence and offers it as a quick solution rather than an unwanted last resort. Recall former United States senator John McCain singing 'Bomb, bomb, bomb, bomb, bomb Iran', a parody to the Regent's song Barbara Ann, during his 2008 presidential campaign. Or consider the current US president, Donald Trump's, casual rhetoric about nuclear war with North Korea. It's not a stretch to say that the political arena is a stage on which male fantasies around power, violence and domination play out. The terrifying consequence being that life-threatening decisions are made on the basis of ego. Male abuse of power is dangerous in any circumstance and we often see it at its most extreme through the political sphere.

Women: Inherently benevolent leaders?

There is a long running sexist joke I recall hearing during my teenagers years: if the majority of world leaders were women, they would be spending their time discussing make-up and clothes. There would be no more war, because rather than fight, women leaders in conflict would just never speak to each other again. Ironic that in the context of this joke, peace is somehow seen as a weaker, feminine trait, and that war, where millions of innocent lives are lost, is perceived as a normal form of conflict resolution; stronger, more masculine and therefore more superior. While it is more complex than I can go into detail here, and conflict resolution requires productive discussion with other countries, in light of everything that is happening in the world right now, countries solving their disputes by never speaking to each other again actually seems like progressive foreign policy, compared to the US' decision to spearhead a military invasion that saw the deaths of over a half a million people.

This conversation does beg the question of what the world would actually look like if the majority of the world's leaders were women. Would there be less war and conflict if the majority of Heads of State, Presidents and Prime Ministers were women? Obviously, there is no way to know until it actually happens. However, people remain divided on the subject. In the same article, 'Would The World Be More Peaceful If There Were More Women Leaders?' medical anthropologist at the University of Yale, Catherine Panter-Brick, claims that assuming the world would be more peaceful is a gender stereotype, while cognitive psychologist at the University of Harvard, Stephen Pinker, argues that throughout history, women have been and will be the pacifying force.[2]

Many arguments about female leaders fail to account for the following question: if the majority of world leaders were women, but they were operating under western imperialism, capitalism and patriarchy, then why assume that anything would change?

2   https://aeon.co/ideas/would-the-world-be-more-peaceful-if-there-were-more-women-leaders (last accessed 05/12/2018).

There would still be an 'Other', so it follows that there would still be conflict and war. In fact, many women leaders have furthered or perpetuated patriarchy in order to be on a level playing field with men, reaching positions of leadership, only to end up exercising power in the same way as the men before them. Take the case of Margaret Thatcher. She was dubbed 'The Iron Lady', and was Britain's first woman Prime Minister, who won three elections with the Conservative Party in 1979, 1983 and 1987. Her popularity was bolstered among Conservative MPs after she led the country to the Falklands war in 1982. Moving forward to the present day, our current prime minister, Theresa May, is accused of facilitating the 'state sponsored abuse of women' through the Yarl's Wood immigration detention centre, while the hostile environment policy introduced by her as Home Secretary resulted in the deportation of hundreds of thousands of migrants, including the Windrush scandal.

Even in the male-dominated corporate world, in particular within senior positions, such as the role of CEO's, women that present more 'masculine' or ruthless traits, prioritising money making over empathy for colleagues, are generally taken more seriously, with more access to success, usually rising to higher ranks. Race and class come into play here: if any women are more likely to be in these positions and replicate the success of men, they are white middle-class women. However, there are problems all women face collectively, and women are very rarely, if at all, are afforded the privilege of presenting 'femininity' in the same way that men are encouraged to present their masculinity within the political and corporate spheres. In 2010, MEP (Member of the European Parliament) Licia Ronzulli of Italy stirred up controversy and faced backlash by bringing along her month-old baby, Vittoria, to a voting session on the working conditions of women at the European Union, Strasbourg.

Men and political extremism

Political power is patriarchal, and patriarchal power is political. Male domination across the political spectrum is about power. Opposing ideological views that are perceived to be on polar ends of the political spectrum often have one thing in common: masculinity. The question of why so many young men are being radicalised, whether through Jihadism, neo-Nazi and White Nationalist movements such as the Alt-right or any other violent male-centred political movement, is one that has been overlooked, particularly in mainstream conversation. In his book *Healing From Hate: How Young Men Get Into – and Out of – Violent Extremism*, Sociologist Michael Kimmel argues that masculinity is the root cause of why so many young men continue to join these violent political movements, and the social glue that keeps so many young men together.

Kimmel argues that the young men involved in these violent political movements have a sense of 'aggrieved entitlement',[3] in that they feel they have not received what they are entitled to, or what they had expected to gain through virtue of being a man. As a result, many men believe their masculinity is under threat, and that they therefore have to take to extreme measures – usually violent ones – to protect it. An example of this is reflected in a *Huffington Post* article, *How Masculinity, Not Ideology, Drives Violent Extremism*. Journalist Dina Temple-Raston features a teenage boy from Minnesota who sold the little he owned (iPhone, trainers and laptop), to book a flight to Turkey, and eventually made his way to Syria to join the Islamic State. The boy said 'I thought I was fighting on the side of an oppressed people . . . I felt like I was going to face another military . . . I

---

3   Michael Kimmel, *Healing from Hate: How Young Men Get Into – And Out Of – Political Extremism* (University of California Press, 2018).

felt like I was doing something noble; it gave me meaning.' The teenage boy was eventually arrested by the FBI and charged with terrorism offences.[4]

On the other side of the political spectrum, we have the rhetoric of the forty-fifth President of the United States, Donald Trump, who used sexist and racist speech to appeal to and bolster support from white American men (and white American women – who constituted 53 per cent of his voter-ship), many of whom felt their entitlement and privilege was slipping away from them. Trump – also nicknamed Ronald McDonald Trump, Agent Orange, and, a personal favourite, Cheeto Benito – in response to the #MeToo movement and the allegations of sexual assault and misconduct levelled at Supreme Court nominee, Judge Kavanagh, said 'It is a very scary time for young men in America.' What Trump is calling scary is the idea of men finally starting to be held accountable for their past and present and actions, where they would have otherwise got away with it (let's be clear: he is talking quite specifically about white men). Being held accountable for their actions is 'scary' to young men in America, where young women in America fear gendered-violence; rape, sexual abuse and harassment. There is no comparison between the two.

Accountability is what someone with entitlement and privilege fears the most because being held accountable for every single one of your actions is the status of the oppressed, dispossessed and disempowered; to be privileged is to not be judged. In a patriarchal society, women are constantly held accountable, to the point where they are aggressively blamed for things that they are not accountable for. Even in the political

---

4   www.washingtonpost.com/outlook/how-masculinity-not-ideology-drives-violent-extremism/2018/03/20/7b223c90-1e29-11e8-b2d908e748f892c0_story.html?noredirect=on&utm_term=.8cb339cb44ae (last accessed 23/03/2019).

realm, so often what a female political leader says and does is under so much more scrutiny. What if a woman had uttered the rhetoric of Donald Trump? It's difficult to confidently say that she would remain in the White House for as long as Trump has, let alone be voted in. This comparison may even be difficult to imagine. We need only go so far as to look at the way in which Hillary Clinton was scrutinised. Although Hillary Clinton is undoubtedly not a politician without fault, she received a lot more scrutiny than Trump received when 'messing up' during her electoral campaign. And Alexandria Ocasio-Cortez, US representative for the Democratic party, faces gendered abuse. Whether men or women are running to be leaders, they are making decisions that affect people across the globe and should be held equally accountable.

More and more men in America are committing political acts of violence today in our current climate, as they have done throughout history. While terrorism constitutes acts of violence in the pursuit of political aims, the media fails to label white supremacist acts of violence carried out by men as acts of terrorism. The media perpetuates the idea that terrorist acts are politically violent acts committed exclusively by Muslim minorities. For example, an act of domestic American terrorism was carried out by the 'Mail Bomber', Cesar Sayoc, who, in October 2018, was charged with making threats and sending explosive devices to prominent Democratic politicians, donors and CNN offices in New York – it's worth mentioning that the violence was aimed at vocal opponents of Donald Trump. These political acts of violence are being labelled as carried out by 'lone rangers'; that is to say, someone who acts alone and is not motivated by political ideology. But how many lone ranger violent attacks does it take before people associate political ideology with them: whether it's white supremacy or gender-based violence, or both, these acts are political and often the violence is brewing in male pacts, as opposed to the picture painted of a lone ranger.

Men across the world are utilising political violence as a means to re-engage with their masculinity, to feel emboldened, to feel 'strong', to feel like what they think it means to be a man; someone who fights for what they believe, someone who would risk a life and/or take a life, to protect what they think is theirs. And in this case, it is the fact of male-entitlement that is being taken away, which leads to this kind of political violence.

The fact is that patriarchy disempowers the majority of men. It is of course a system that grants men privilege, however, it is not beneficial to the majority of men. Only an elite few, the upper class of men truly benefit from patriarchy, as we will discuss in Chapters 6 and 7. The rest, essentially, have to battle it out for the scraps that remain – which is usually an illusion or false sense of entitlement; a feeling of privilege and a false sense of superiority; particularly in politics, as it is never those who decide the wars and political conflicts that are the same ones fighting and dying in them. However, as much as patriarchy disempowers men, it disempowers women to a greater degree. And so many men hold on to that entitlement and privilege, as a means of feeling superior to another person. It is like being trapped in a burning house, but not panicking or looking for an escape because you aren't yet on fire.

Chapter 5

If I were a boy: Gender equality and feminism

'Feminism is the radical notion that women are human beings', wrote Marie Shear, writer, editor and political activist, in the *New Directions for Women* newsletter back in 1986. On the surface, this seems to be a straightforward claim, hence the irony detectable in the words 'radical notion'. People often respond to a statement like this in one of two ways. Some will argue: 'of course women are human beings', without taking into consideration – or even being aware of – the systematic and structural oppression that women face within a patriarchal society, which essentially positions them as inferior to men, and therefore lesser human beings. The second response will likely be to agree that women are human beings, but accounting for the fact that while objectively that is the case, it is not reflected in society.

When I was a young teenager in the late 90s and early 2000s, I was completely unaware of gender equality on a structural level, which we will discuss in this chapter. I was aware of gender roles and expectations, and the supposed differences between men and women, which largely went unchallenged around me. However, I grew up in a household with a mother and father, and five boys. My mother made sure we all cooked and cleaned because she believed that it was important for us to contribute to housework, regardless of gender. I grew up watching my father go to work and my mum work as a stay-at-home mum. At other times, I watched my mum go to work and my dad as the stay-at-home dad.

Back then, I thought everyone grew up the same way I did. As I got older, I slowly came to see that the fact that I cooked and cleaned was viewed as exemplary for a man, and outside of the norm. Many of the men I knew were unenthusiastic about doing housework, to say the least, and expected the closest girl they had in their lives, whether best friend, girlfriend or even mother, to do it for them. These expectations that women have to perform their 'duty', is just one of the many things that validates treating women as lesser human beings, and more so, as objects, particularly objects of service. This experience opened my eyes, and I was always filled with questions about why or why not boys or girls could do certain things. I was told by most people, 'that's just the way it is'. But it was reading books on gender equality and feminism that really brought me the answers to the most pressing questions I had on gender.

What is feminism?

I read bell hooks' *Feminism is for Everybody* as a late teenager, and it answered a lot of the questions that I had about gender equality and feminism. I realised that if someone had asked if I wanted to end sexism, sexist exploitation and oppression, that I would agree. But if someone asked me if I was a feminist, or if I agreed with feminism, then I would hesitate, or probably at least at that time disagree. This revealed more about how the ideology was represented by people, than the ideology itself. Feminism is often posited as an anti-male ideology; as a movement that essentially seeks to rid the world of men, as men are the inherent problem in society. In *Feminism is for Everybody*, academic and activist, bell hooks, writes: 'Simply put, feminism is a movement to end sexism, sexist exploitation, and oppression. I liked this definition because it does not imply that men were the enemy.'[1]

hook's vision of feminism is inherently tied to the structural and systematic oppression of women in society. While many men are aware of gender norms and expectations, as they see them play out in their everyday lives, as I was as a teenager, they aren't aware of why feminism is still necessary in the modern world, considering it an antiquated idea – a throwback to women getting the vote, or exclusively being housewives. Think of the following retort: 'But our prime minister is a woman.' However, women are still very much oppressed in modern society, in particular, working-class women of colour. Here are some global statistics from UN Women:[2]

- Women are more likely to be unemployed than men
- Globally, women are paid less than men. The gender wage gap is estimated to be 23 per cent
- Women bear disproportionate responsibility for unpaid care and domestic work
- Women are less likely to have access to social protection: globally, an estimated nearly 40 per cent of women in wage employment do not have access to social protection
- Environmental degradation and climate change have disproportionate impacts on women and children: globally women are 40 times more likely than men to die during a disaster
- Many migrant women participate in low-skilled and precarious jobs characterised by low wages, poor working

---

1   bell hooks, *Feminism Is For Everybody* (Pluto Press, 2000).

2   www.unwomen.org/en/what-we-do/economic-empowerment/facts-and-figures.

conditions, limited labour and social protections, and exposure to physical and sexual violence

Male privilege

I don't know that men are so willing to sacrifice. As men, if we accept that we have status and power and privilege, are men prepared to sacrifice that? Are men prepared to give that up? I know some sacrificial women, so I don't know if men are willing to give that up? – Adam

Male privilege refers to the social, economic and political advantages and rights that are made available to men as a result of their sex. Feminism is perceived as being against men or a threat to men, because it centres on women's struggles. Many men have an automatic knee-jerk reaction to this, fearing that their freedom is going to be taken away from them. But feminism is simply about levelling the playing field and creating a world where women are not more likely to suffer, or even die – as the above statistics reveal – by virtue of being a woman. Feminists such as hooks do not want to shift these adverse situations on to men, but want to eliminate the chances of this happening to any human being.

Not only do feminists want to create a more equal society for women, they have also fought for the rights of men. Feminism is actually beneficial to men as it seeks to heal men and remove the pressures that patriarchal society places on them, particularly the false assertions and impositions of masculinity, and the general political and social destruction patriarchy can cause: a destruction that causes a lot of men to have mental health breakdowns, and is seen as largely connected to the alarming rate at which men are committing suicide.

On his album podcast Prometheus Vol. 3, released in August 2018, the popular, internationally recognised Scottish comedian, Frankie Boyle, says the following about feminism:

I'm going to tell you honestly what I think about feminism . . . I genuinely think, if you're a young guy at the moment, feminism is the only thing that has a plan for you. Capitalism doesn't give a fuck about you, materialism doesn't really care if you live or die. Feminism includes you. And when I see guys, particularly young guys, attacking feminism, do you know what it looks like to me? It looks like when the Fire Brigade go to a really rough housing estate, and they get stoned. That's what you're doing, you're stoning the fucking rescue services.

When more women are in employment, and when men and women are paid equally for the same labour, not only does it boost the economy, it removes the financial pressure of the man being the sole provider (a role prescribed under patriarchy) and gives more autonomy to both men and women. Many do not know, that feminist activists' launched the campaign in 2011: *Rape is Rape* pressuring the FBI and demanding a new definition that reflected the realities of rape, including the sexual violence that boys and men experience – the previous definition was unchanged since 1929. And Black feminists have notoriously fought for the rights of Black men. Audre Lorde wrote:

I wish to raise a Black man who will not be destroyed by, nor settle for, those corruptions called *power* by the white fathers who mean his destruction as surely as they mean mine. I wish to raise a Black man who will recognize that the legitimate objects of his hostility are not women, but the particulars of a structure that programs him to fear and despise women as well as his own Black self.[3]

Men: Predators or protectors?

In many ways, men know that society is different for men and women: that men pose a threat to women, and that power dynamics are constantly at play in everyday life. It is subtly reinforced in our outward performances of masculinity. When it comes to the girls or women in our lives, including sisters, nieces, cousins, mothers, often a defensive and protective instinct is at play. Popular culture, including films, plays a role in reflecting the male psyche, and the dichotomy of men as 'predators' and women as damsels in distress to be protected. I recall a scene from the film *Bad Boys II* (2003), featuring Will Smith and Martin Lawrence, as Police Detectives Mike Lowrey and Marcus Burnett. A boy named Reggie comes to take Marcus Burnett's daughter, Megan, on a date. Reggie knocks on the door and Detective Burnett slams the door open. The scene goes as follows:

Detective Burnett: Who the f*** are you?
Reggie: Hi, Mr. Bennett. I'm Reggie.
Detective Burnett: What you doing here?
Reggie: I came to take out Megan.
Detective Burnett: How old are you?
Reggie: I'm 15, Mr. Burnett.
Detective Burnett: M****r f****r you look 30.

Detective Burnett then pushes Reggie against the wall and pats him down for a search. Detective Mike Lowrey then arrives. Lowrey continues with the same inquisition as Bennett.

---

3   Audre Lorde, *Sister Outsider: Essays and Speeches* (Ten Speed Press, 2007).

Detective Lowrey: Can you fight?
Reggie: Yeah.
Detective Lowrey: You can fight? (Lowrey then fakes as if he is going to hit Reggie).

You can't fight.

Detective Burnett: Mike, Mike . . .
Detective Lowrey: No. If someone is going to take my niece out, I wanna know if the [redacted] can fight. Someone might come and say something, if the [redacted] can't fight, then she can't go.
Detective Burnett: This is Megan's godfather. He just got out of the joint (prison).
Detective Lowrey: (pulls out gun and starts waving it in the air) I just got out of jail and I ain't going back. What's wrong with you (to Reggie)? You acting all scared, you ain't ever seen a gun before?

. . .

Detective Burnett: Have my daughter home at 10.01(pm). If she ain't home at 10.01, I'm in the car, locked and loaded, and I'm hunting your m***** f****** a** down.

Then the wife of Detective Burnett, Theresa Burnett, comes to the door with Megan, and happily greets Reggie, welcoming him and excusing the detectives for their silly behaviour. Before Reggie walks into the house, Detective Burnett whispers to Reggie:

Detective Burnett: Are you a virgin?
Reggie: Yeah.

Detective Burnett: Good. Keep it that way. Ain't gonna be no f*****g tonight!

I remember watching this particular scene as a teenager with my brothers and my male friends, and joking about how we would emulate this kind of male protectionism over our hypothetical, unborn daughters. Interactions such as these suggest that men implicitly know that other men pose a danger: particularly a man who they do not know or have not verified as an 'acceptable' male – Reggie in the scene from *Bad Boys*. In the small excerpt, Burnett and Lowrey make references to the looks, fighting abilities and sexuality of a 15-year-old boy. In this way, men often view the male identity as encompassing both 'predator and protector'. The problem is that while many men are aware of gender inequality, they are invested in the male privilege afforded to them, which means that wanting to protect women – usually those in their family, as the *Bad Boys* scene reflects – is not necessarily synonymous with wanting to evaluate the role that they might play in perpetuating misogyny. If men want to make the world a safer space for their loved ones, they must be awakened to women's humanity, not only to women in their family.

Male feminists?

The question of whether men should identify as feminists is a hotly debated one. As a man, understanding the essential principles of feminism and the issue of gender equality is arguably more important than labelling oneself a feminist. As explored in this chapter, feminism as an ideology is linked to harmful oppressive structures, which harm men as well as women. Feminism cares more about men than any other male movement that may exist out there, such as Men's Rights Movements: MRA's (Men's

Rights Activists) are notably anti-feminist, with members claiming that 'Young men should be furious' about feminism,[4] encouraging aggressive mindsets among men, in contrast to feminism which encourages men to be freed of this toxicity.

A self-identifying male feminist may give off a number of impressions. Often, when a man identifies as a feminist, other men look down on him; to a certain degree, it emasculates a man among men. Some men (and some women) view men who identify as feminists as trying to win over women by pretending to care. Among some women, a self-identifying male feminist is often uplifted and immediately identified as an ally; sometimes self-identifying feminist men take advantage of that. In the wake of the #MeToo movement, many women publicly shared their experiences of being taken advantage of by men: it was clear that this wasn't exclusively by men who were openly misogynistic or hostile to women, but often by men who identified as feminists. This is part of the reason I don't necessarily identify as feminist, or feel that men have to. Men should not be rewarded for doing the basic, fundamental thing of treating women, people, as human beings. That should be the point at which we start the conversation, not the apex of it. Men must also work with or among other men to dismantle the patriarchy and reject toxic masculinity: when bell hooks argued that 'feminism is for everybody', she highlighted the fact that feminism is not only women's work, nor does it only benefit women. Women are not fighting to take anything away from men: rather they are fighting to re-balance and reimagine a world without inequality. It is important for us to understand that having a society with a fair and equal gender balance, in terms of rights, access, treatment, benefits and more, is something that we should all strive for.

---

4   www.opendemocracy.net/en/5050/young-men-should-be-furious-inside-worlds-largest-mens-rights-activism/ (last accessed 14/03/2019).

Chapter 6

See you at the cross-roads: Intersections of masculinity

> It's a fiction, this thing of . . . you are a man, so you are like this . . . one of the things I'm starting to understand is there is no man or woman, you're just a being with lots of parts within you . . . I guess, the idea of a 'man', for me, is becoming less and less important. – Ned

Men are different from women, but men are also different from men. When we think of a 'man' a number of common images may arise in our collective imagination. For example, perhaps someone who is tall, athletic, with broad shoulders, a deep voice, a particular ethnicity or sexuality – which in the mainstream, at least, tends to be a straight white man. We often project onto that man our ideas of what he should look and act like, and everything else is a deviation from that norm. Given that we live in a world of 7 billion plus people, approximately 3.5 billion of whom are men, there cannot and should not be any one way that men should be. Cultures and ideologies that have dominated over another and imposed their beliefs and understandings on other nations and cultures, attempting to create a globalised, singular worldview of manhood. Being a man is not a standardised test that men take, with a median pass rate that men either fall above or below. Rather than there being a norm of manhood, people should have the open mindedness and understanding to realise that there are beautiful variations of manhood and masculinity, and that however the male identity might manifest, that does not make that person more or less of a man.

The Axes of Oppression

When analysing how the structure of society impacts the lives of its citizens based on their identities, often only one identity is considered. For example, when looking at women's experiences, we often only see gender, or we only see sexuality when looking at gay people's experiences: these are the first things that come to mind. But various parts of our identity change the way society treats us, as they relate to how society's systems impact us. Parts of our identity overlap, some giving us an advantage or privilege, while other parts oppress us and form obstacles or barriers in many ways. Feminist, Kimberlé Crenshaw coined the term 'intersectionality' to describe how institutions of oppression intersect to oppress women of colour in society: we can use this idea about the various axes of oppression to explore the different positions men have in society.

As a young Black, working-class, university educated, straight man living in London, I am privileged as a male; I am privileged to be university educated; and to live in London. However, the global prevalence of racism means that I am treated differently because of my race – this can range from systematic disadvantages to people's perceptions of me. I grew up and live in London, so this gives me access to more opportunities for employment compared to someone living, for example, in the northeast of England: an area that has been underfunded for decades and has one of the highest unemployment rates in the UK. However, being a refugee largely negatively impacted my reality; I did not have legal status and I was refused and denied access to many things, for example, travel and education. I identify as a man, and I am an able-bodied man. Therefore generally, I don't have to worry about travelling around on public transport and having to choose a different station because the closest one is not accessible for wheelchair users, as men with physical disabilities have to. There would also have to be other considerations to take into account if I were a gay man, or a trans man, or middle-class or privately educated and so forth. To reiterate, each person's identity comes with a different set of privileges or challenges – and a lot of that is based on the structure and system of society. It's not to say that life is inherently more or less challenging if you have one aspect of an identity or another. It's also not productive to make it sound like some kind of comparative better-off/worse-off oppression Olympics, which is limited in its analysis. But nuance is essential when understanding how our experiences differ as a result of our identities, and what that tells us about the hierarchal structures of society. This structural analysis is emphasised by Crenshaw when she coined intersectionality as a '. . . process of recognising as social and systemic what was formerly perceived as isolated and individual'.[1] Ultimately, men are men, and patriarchy is patriarchy. However, the goal posts shift based on race, class, sexuality and so forth. When it is 'men' who are being referred to as a majority or group, it is important to also look at the distinctions between men.

---

1 Kimberlé Williams Crenshaw, *Maping the Margins: Intersectionality, Identity Politics and Violence Against Women of Colour*, www.jstor.org/stable/1229039?seq=1#page_scan_tab_contents (last accessed 20/03/2019).

Class

Class is still a major point of division around the world today: society is made up of separate classes, including the elite class in power, the middle class and the working class. Often, economic status is conflated with perception when discussing class. For example, someone who is wealthy drives a nice car and lives in a big house, may be seen as middle-class. However, if that person is a young footballer who grew up in the inner city (and talks in a working-class inner city accent of a particular region), people may think of them as working-class. Whereas someone who attends the Opera or theatre, just by virtue of attending or engaging in these social and cultural activities, could be seen as middle-class or labelled as such, but they could in fact be working in a call centre or a job that pays the living wage or just below it. Class can impact how people are treated when it comes to people's perceptions of your class, but the reality of one's class also dictates economic circumstances and living situations, from lack of access to education, housing, social protection, employment, and healthcare.

Working-class men, almost exclusively white working-class men, are often caricatured and stereotyped as 'chavs', 'cockneys', 'lads', associated with the kind of culture that involves excessive alcohol consumption, aggression and violent behaviour. Think Del Boy x Phil Mitchell x Danny Dyer; think going down the market x having a quick punch up x going to the pub. In *Chavs: the Demonisation of the Working-Class*, Owen Jones writes about these harmful stereotypes, which are breathed with new life by the media as well as the state, as an 'overlapping series of chav caricatures: the feckless, the non-aspirational, the scrounger, the dysfunctional and the disorderly'.[2] The connotations of

---

2   Owen Jones, *Chavs: The Demonisation of the Working Class* (Verso, 2016).

working-class men are rarely positive. Rarely do people associate them with intelligence, education or achievement (outside of sport). This is perceived to be a personal failure, but if we look at the research we see that the barriers they face are societal failure. In the book, *Miseducation: Inequality, Education and the Working Classes*, Professor Reay found that in the UK, around 18 per cent of English school education spending goes to the 7 per cent of pupils who are privately educated, while the Organisation for Economic Cooperation and Development report in 2013 concluded that schools in England are among the most socially segregated in the developed world.[3]

Working-class masculinity is often considered dangerous in its own right, in that any violence or aggression or sexist language and behaviour is seen as unique to being working-class. The picture painted of middle-class masculinity – and middle-class-ness more generally – is very different. Ideas of men that are intellectual, cultured, and therefore inherently less harmful emerges. Not only is this a classist myth, but it's a myth that results in men using their elite status to abuse their power and for it to go unseen. A friend of mine, with a working-class family background, described his experience in a private education boarding school, as more toxic than his upbringing and prior environments in terms of male peer pressure and performative masculine rituals. He felt his masculinity was under pressure and out of place in this environment. A lot of private education institutions, independent schools, boarding schools and universities are harbouring grounds for toxic masculine behaviours, including misogynistic cultures. In 2018, eleven students from the University of Warwick – one of the UK's top universities – were suspended for sexist (and racist) messages sent in a group

---

3   Diane Reay, *Miseducation: Inequality, Education and the Working Classes* (Policy Press, 2017).

chat, which included 'rape her friends too', 'sometimes it's fun to just go wild and rape 100 girls', and 'rape the whole flat to teach them all a lesson'.[4]

Race

Today, the far right continues to spread the myth that the working-class is exclusively white. However, the statistics paint a very different picture. The TUC report on Insecure Work and Ethnicity found that Black and Minority Ethnic (BAME) groups are persistently disadvantaged in the labour market: one in three BAME employees are in insecure work, and one in eight Black employees are in insecure work, the average is one in seventeen.[5] If you bring race into the working-class identity, and a man becomes a working-class Black man, there immediately arises a whole new set of systematic challenges, and provocations, stereotypes and connotations. Black men, in the West in particular, are criminalised and hypersexualised, by simple virtue of being Black. Black men are overrepresented in the criminal justice system, often for lower level crimes, and in many cases, Black men get longer sentences than white men for the same crime. A report by the US sentencing commission found that Black men got 19.1 per cent longer sentences for the same federal crimes between fiscal years 2012 and 2016.[6] Black men are also more likely to be stopped and searched by police than white men. A Gov.UK research report on stop and search

---

4 www.bbc.co.uk/news/uk-england-coventry-warwickshire-44052070 (last accessed 05/03/2019).

5 www.tuc.org.uk/sites/default/files/Insecure%20work%20and%20ethnicity_0. pdf (last accessed 20/03/2019).

6 www.ussc.gov/research/research-reports/demographic-differences-sentencing (last accessed 20/03/2019).

found that in 2017–18 in England and Wales, Black people were nine and a half times more likely to be stopped and searched by the police than white people.[7]

There have been several occasions during my teenage years and as an adult where I have been stopped by the police for looking 'suspicious', or fitting a certain description, while doing ordinary things that people do every day, such as making my way home or going to the shops. The authorities, as well civilians, treat you with particular suspicion if they see you occupying a space where they do not expect you to be. I have been stopped so many times, whether by security or by people, when I am going into a particular institution or organisation, especially where I have been the guest speaker or facilitator. The surprised look on people's faces when I come forward is the same everywhere I go. There is also the stereotypical 'roadman', 'gangster' or 'hood/ ghetto' association related to drugs and crime that is associated with Black men. I have been asked so many times whether I sell drugs or know where I can get some drugs by non-Black people. I usually get asked for cannabis/weed, which is ironic because the number one cannabis/weed smoking country in the world is Iceland, with 18.3 per cent of its population smoking the drug,[8] and they aren't even remotely close to being stereotyped or associated with the drug.

Sexuality

The relationship between sexuality and masculinity has a long and complex history, remaining a major point of tension in the

---

7   www.ethnicity-facts-figures.service.gov.uk/crime-justice-and-the-law/policing/ stop-and-search/latest.
8   www.telegraph.co.uk/travel/maps-and-graphics/mapped-the-countries-that- smoke-the-most-cannabis (last accessed 07/03/2019).

male identity. Gay men, and even femme straight men, face threats and often even suffer violence at the hands of homophobic straight men in society. A Pew Research Centre survey in the US states that 92 per cent of LGBTQ adults saw society as becoming more accepting over the last decade (2003–13), yet only 55 per cent of those surveyed had a favourable view of gay men compared to 37 per cent in 2003.[9] The US is a place that is considered generally more progressive and accepting of its views on sexuality compared to other places in the world, for example, Uganda, where homosexuality is still criminalised, but homophobia is still a central part of the fabric of Western society.

Gay men are often seen as weaker men, who are deviants of masculinity. Furthermore, men are not afforded sexual fluidity. When it comes to male sexuality you are often either straight, or not-straight (gay); queer or bi-sexual men are often erased from the spectrum of male sexuality. However, while women being openly fluid with their sexuality is more acceptable – think 'I-Kissed-a-girl-and-I-liked-it' – this is also a by-product of the patriarchy, and often makes gay or queer female relationships about male fantasy. Taboo around queer and bisexual men can mean they are pushed away from both men and women who consider them not to be man enough in different ways. In a society where men are overwhelmingly violent towards other men, a man loving another man is a radical, progressive act. How does it make any sense that we, as a society, are more accepting of male violence than we are of male love? Male love should be normalised, as a way to combat male violence.

I had deep shame, because I was looking at what I was looking at and I had no one around me that I knew who was gay . . .

9 www.pewresearch.org/fact-tank/2013/06/25/how-lgbt-adults-see-society-and-how-the-public-sees-them (last accessed 20/01/2019).

and all I could think of was: why am I not like all the men around me? That was scary, I beat myself up for years.

I do find being a gay man around straight men, they find that friendship as a sort of outlet to be more emotional and reveal that side of them that they wouldn't normally do with their (straight) friends. And so I built friendships with straight men and it's a completely different dynamic. – Elrick

Trans and gender fluidity

Colonialism – the total political, economic and cultural exploitation and domination of one nation over another – has been one of the most significant factors in shaping the way sexuality is viewed throughout history and today, particularly in the Global South, Africa, Asia, South America and the Middle East (often referred to as the 'Third World' or 'developing countries'). Colonialism eventually led to the criminalisation of homosexuality in many of these countries, particularly African countries such as Uganda, Nigeria, Zimbabwe, with countries such as Sudan and Mauritania even implementing the death penalty. The reason colonialism was so impactful was because it came with religious imperialism, the missionaries who converted people to Christianity and/or Islam, meanwhile erasing the way of life and beliefs that were practised and held on to before. Homosexuality was practised in Africa long before European conquest, says author and novelist Bernadine Evaristo, who references rock paintings of the San people of Zimbabwe that shows anal sex between men. Evaristo also argues that it was in fact homophobia that was imported into Africa – prior to this, sexuality was seen as something that was fluid and free, between all genders.[10]

10 www.theguardian.com/commentisfree/2014/mar/08/african-homosexuality-colonial-import-myth (last accessed 20/01/2019).

In pre-colonial societies across the world, sexuality and gender were fluid, free and not limited to strict binaries. For instance, the Hijra people are trans gender and intersex people who live in India and South Asia, and have done so for centuries. They are officially recognised in many of these countries, such as Nepal, Pakistan, India or Bangladesh, as being neither male nor female, but a third gender. I attended a literature festival in Kerala, India, where I was among many writers from all over the world. One evening, during dinner with the group, I spoke with an older gentleman; a professor from an elite UK university. The subject was gender fluidity and how India had changed its laws to legally recognise a third gender. His response was 'Finally, it's good to see India showing some progress after being backwards for so long.' I was shocked to hear him say this, especially considering how educated he was. I replied 'Actually, gender fluidity was quite a normal concept in India centuries ago, until the British came and colonised it out of them.' He had no response, he only mumbled himself into silence.

The concept of more genders than the typical male-female binary is also a large part of Native American culture and society, where up to five genders are recognised. Professor of anthropology and gender at the University of Southern California, Walter L. Williams, writes that Native Americans usually held intersex, androgynous, feminine males and masculine females in high respect in their society, and that the most common term to define such a person is 'two-spirit'.[11]

In my Congolese culture, and across many cultures around the world, historically, gender fluid or trans gender people were often held to an elevated status in society or were seen as higher spiritual beings, creative in the arts, song and dance. In

---

11   Walter Williams, *Two-Spirit People: Native American Gender Identity, Sexuality, and Spirituality* (University of Illinois Press, 1997).

the pre-colonial Kingdom of Kongo, circa the fifteenth century, the concept of gender was illustrated through a popular creation story, which said that the original human was the perfect being that descended onto the earth from the heavens, named *Kimahungu*, who was both feminine and masculine, both man and woman. It populated the earth by multiplying itself and spreading around the world. Congolese historian, theologian and professor, Dr Kiatezua Lubanzadio, writes about this extensively.[12] Many of these theologies have been erased as a result of colonialism (which branded it as evil, pagan or backwards). However, there are remnants of these ideas that still exist in modern Congo culture. For instance, in Lingala (one of the four main languages spoken in DR Congo), the left hand is called *Liboko ya mwasi*, and the right hand is called *Liboko ya mobali*, meaning the woman's hand, the man's hand, respectively. This is a symbolic representation of both the feminine and masculine in each person, as originally conceived in the *Kimahungu* myth of the Kongo people.

The reality for gender fluid, non-binary or trans gender people in modern society, however, is far from an elevated status. Rather, they face the risk of ridicule, exclusion, marginalisation, and often violence or death. Violence against trans gender people is on the rise across the world. There were 369 reported murders of trans gender people around the world, the majority of these happening in Brazil, as well as Mexico, the United States, and Colombia. In the United States, the majority killed were trans women of colour and/or Native American trans women.[13] Not to mention the fact that many trans gender people experience

---

12 Dr Kiatezua Lubanzadio Luyaluka, *La Religion Kongo: Ses Origines Egyptiennes et Sa Convergence Avec La Christianisme* (Editions L'Harmattan, 2000).

13 https://transrespect.org/en/tmm-update-trans-day-of-remembrance-2018/ (last accessed 26/01/2019).

violence and abuse that they do not report to the authorities –
often out of fear of being further attacked or ridiculed by the
authorities, where transphobia is often rife: this means that the
number of attacks on trans gender people is certainly higher than
what we see reflected in statistics. In July 2017, President Trump
tweeted that trans gender individuals would not be allowed to
serve in the military, while the Department of Justice has rolled
back protections for transgender inmates that were put in place
by President Obama.

> My journey into identifying as gender non-conforming was
> something that I felt, and then the language caught up. – Tom

The concept of gender and sexual fluidity can be a difficult
reality to grasp within a world that imposes heteronormative
strict gender binaries. I was raised in a religious background:
Congolese/African culture is very religious, with Christianity
dominating in the sub-Saharan region in particular. The notion
of gender or sexual fluidity was taught to me as abhorrent or
deviant from the way that the world was created or meant to be,
long before I even developed a sexual orientation of my own;
imagine being a five year old boy who is told that any boy who
likes another boy will burn in hell forever – it is a terrifying
thought. When I eventually removed myself from what I was
taught and began to read into spiritual and religious beliefs
that existed before Christianity, or other Abrahamic faiths, and
pre-colonial societies, I learned of just how normal and accepted
gender and sexual fluid people were in more ancient societies,
and how it is not something to be confused by. Often, people
hold on to binary and rigid perceptions of gender and sexuality
because it reinforces their heteronormative identity and their
beliefs in the patriarchal hierarchy. They see gender and sexual

fluidity as a threat to the norm; a threat to themselves. However, there is slow progress being made as gender fluid and trans gender people are becoming more visible and better represented in the mainstream media and society. For example, American actress Amandla Stenberg, identifies as non-binary, using *they* or *them* pronouns (rather than he or she) and has spoken out about the importance of this. Laverne Cox, actress and trans gender woman, in an interview with *Time* magazine, spoke out about her experiences, saying, 'People need to be willing to let go of what they think they know about what it means to be a man and what it means to be a woman. Because that doesn't neces-sarily mean anything inherently.' When asked what she thinks makes people so uncomfortable with the trans identity, she replies '. . . people don't want to critically interrogate the world around them. Whenever I'm afraid of something or threatened by something, it's because it brings up some sort of insecurity in me.'[14]

The way we view the world and the people within it is shaped significantly by many factors such as culture, religious and spiritual beliefs, our individual experiences, as well as the era that we are born into. What was normal 800 years ago in a pre-colonial society may not be seen as normal in a modern westernised global world today, and vice versa. What remains is that nothing is ever absolute or permanent; that beliefs change, norms change, ideas change. Perhaps the way we view gender and sexuality in the modern day needs to change as well. There is no one way to be a man, just as there is no one way to be a woman, or no one way to be non-binary. When we impose fixed notions on ourselves or on other people, we limit our potential

---

14   Katy Steinmez, 'Laverne Cox Talks to TIME About the Transgender Movement,' *Time* (2014), http://time.com/132769/transgender-orange-is-the-new-black-laverne-cox-interview (last accessed 26/01/2019).

to feel comfortable as our true selves and we also risk alienation. What remains is the necessity to understand each other's lived experiences, learning from the realities of others who are the same as us but also from those who are different to us. This enables us to grow and gain a greater understanding of all people so that we can fight for a world where people are not marginalised for being themselves.

Chapter 7

It goes down in the DMs: Masculinity in the age of social media

Social media and social networking platforms have allowed our generation to create external representations of our idealised internal identities and lives. Videos, images, memes, tags, and tweets dominate, and in turn, we follow other people who project their ideal representation of self, both of us believing the other's representations to be their reality. The early social media and networking sites of the first decade of the 2000s, such as My Space, Hi5, Bebo, MSN Messenger and chatrooms – which were all uniquely web based – did not have the modern day accessibility of a smartphone-based app, and were limited in terms of connectivity. You had to sit down at a PC to post on social media, which limited the number of users logged on at the same time. In 2018, some of the largest social media platforms, including Facebook, YouTube, Instagram and Twitter, boast a usership of 2.23 billion, 1.8 billion, 1 billion, and 335 million respectively. China, the most populated country in the world, has a population of 1.4 billion people, India has 1.3 billion, the United States has 333 million, Nigeria has 185 million, and Mexico and Japan have

127 million each. The UK has a population of 65 million. When we consider this, one could argue that Facebook is the largest digital country in the world.

If a social media platform was a country, then, just like all countries, it would have its own culture; its norms, values, beliefs and ideas that emerge and spread internally, and externally to present its ideas to the wider world. Social media platforms do have this. And they, much like citizens of a country, have had their own way of spreading these ideas among their users.

#Masculinitysofragile

Across all social media platforms, particular revelatory representations of masculinity shared in a single post would otherwise take a lengthy time to find out about a person. For example, on Twitter, in a tweet which posed the question, 'how fragile is your masculinity?' one twitter user replied:

I was at the gym with this guy and we were doing shoulder exercises using a 15kg bar. He saw a woman doing the same exercise as us with the same weight. This guy turned to me and said, 'I will not use the same weight as that woman.' He added an extra kg.

Another social media post shows a text message exchange between a man and woman that reads:

Man – were you at the Taylor Swift concert?
Woman – yesss haha
Man – great show lol
Woman – omg yes. You've seen it?
Man – I'm not gay but yes

As facetious as these tweets are, they do give us an insight into what people today are labelling a 'fragile' masculinity. However, some experiences of masculinity shared online are more insidious. For example, the following tweet appeared under the hashtag #failingmasculinity: '(my) Mom died when I was 10. Her dad wouldn't hug me or my brothers when we cried. "Men don't hug other men."'

Body image

Modern masculinity has been shaped through the digital realm. Whether through Instagram, Snapchat or YouTube, we are all being presented with a particular type of image and lifestyle. Typically, body image is seen as an issue that women and girls are almost exclusively effected by – research has shown that exposure to ideal female images negatively influences women's self-perception and self-esteem. Many marketing and advertising industries deploy sexist campaigns targeted at young women: groups such as Level Up, challenge sexist media and marketing with counter campaigns. However, there has been less research into the ways in which images influence men's self-perception. Statistics show, for example, in the UK, there has been a rise of 43 per cent in the number of men being referred by their doctors for body image issues and eating disorders in the last two years.[1]

A *Men's Health* (USA) magazine survey of 100 men on body confidence and social media conducted in 2017, indicated that one in three men felt pressure to look good on social platforms. 45 per cent felt pressure to edit or crop pictures to look better, with 46 per cent taking multiple selfies to get the right one. Additionally, one in twenty men reported that they have been

---

1   https://oceanfrontrecovery.com/is-social-media-having-the-same-effect-on-mens-body-image-as-it-is-on-women/ (last accessed 05/12/2018).

teased, trolled or body-shamed on social media about their appearance or weight.[2]

Picture Instagram, and you think of chiselled men with Adonis-like bodies. Bodies which usually only professional athletes have, suddenly seems easily achievable for the average boy after a few gym sessions, protein shakes, and diets. An ideal body type becomes something that can be achieved through 'hard work', without considering crucial other factors, such as being able-bodied or disabled, genetic make-up, class and access to wealth. But perhaps most importantly, we forget that it is absolutely okay to not have chiselled, washboard abs, on a Baywatch, 1000 likes on Instagram, type body.

In an article on male body image from the Michigan University of School of Journalism, bodybuilder Abe Oloko says,

Now more than ever, men are pressured to be the ideal man and body image is obviously attached to it . . . Back in the day, it didn't really matter. A man was looked at for what he could do and provide as a man, but now it's more what you look like.

In the same article, trainer and fitness instructor Phil Williams adds that when he asks a client what they're hoping to gain from personal training, he usually gets shown a picture of some guy on social media 'every time.' He continues, 'It's misrepresenting how people actually are and how fitness should be perceived.'[3] Instagram relies upon editing and filtering, it's dependent on lighting, angles, position, and often promotes a body elitism that is for the majority highly unachievable. Going to the gym

---

2   www.menshealth.com/trending-news/a19542923/body-issues-poll-men (last accessed 05/12/2018).

3   https://news.jrn.msu.edu/2017/12/male-body-image-pressure-increases-with-influence-from-social-media (last accessed 05/12/2018).

to exercise and for fitness is not in and of itself a negative. It is beneficial to a lot of men, including myself, to help with alleviating stress and getting into a healthier mental and physical state. But when the root of that desire for fitness develops into an unhealthy or obsessive goal based on achieving an altered, near impossible to achieve body image, our self-esteem can be lowered and manifest in toxicity. It can create ultra-competitiveness among men – walk into any gym and just observe the environment.

Social media platforms have also had a significant influence on materialism, and the pressures that come with this. Materialism encourages attaching a lot of importance to money, fuelling a desire to possess a lot of things. A 2017 study from Ruhr-University Bochum in Germany, on materialism and social media use, 'Materialists Collect Facebook Friends And Spend More Time On Social Media', found that materialistic people use Facebook more frequently, as it allows them to objectify their Facebook friends and make social comparisons.[4] Comparing oneself with others can be at the root of feelings of personal inadequacy or low self-esteem; if you are constantly shown that you do not have enough, and that everyone else has more – especially if it seems like wealth and material things are easily acquired – you feel as though there is something wrong with you for lacking these possessions. This can leave you feeling pressured to constantly acquire more to be happy – a notion at the heart of capitalist society, which has been linked to mental health problems.

With these social media platforms, we have seen the rise of lifestyle 'influencers'; you can watch them jet setting on private planes and staying in fancy hotels, falsely advertising the now

4   www.elsevier.com/about/press-releases/research-and-journals/materialists-collect-facebook-friends-and-spend-more-time-on-social-media (last accessed 05/03/2019).

infamous Fyre Festival, while luxury brands such as Balenciaga and Christian Louboutin are in demand among the average person. When I was a teenager in the early 2000s, we were not the main audience being targeted or advertised to. This has significantly changed today, particularly with the influence and emergence of 'hype beast' subculture. A hype beast is someone who is obsessed about fashion hype and obtaining the latest styles and trends. UK consultation and professional services network, Deloitte, conducted a piece of research on millennials (18–34 year olds) and spending on luxury brands called 'Bling It On'. In response to the question 'how interested are you in high-end fashion or luxury items (an item that is not deemed necessary)?' over 63 per cent responded 'very interested'. And in response to the question, 'how do you find out about the latest high-end fashion or luxury item trends?' Over 20 per cent replied by social media; 15 per cent stating the brand's website, and 14 per cent stating fashion magazines. On a survey of over a thousand people, Y Pulse, a youth marketing and millennial research firm, concluded the top 20 most wanted luxury brands among 13–34 year olds were (in no particular order): Apple, Tesla, Michael Kors, Louis Vuitton, Rolex, Ferrari and Christian Louboutin, among others.[5]

Twitter trolls and misogyny

The digital revolution and the rise of social media usage have also coincided with a significant increase in online misogyny in recent years. Many people, and men in particular, hide behind anonymous Twitter handles and create 'troll' accounts so that they cannot be identified, using their anonymity to target and

---

5   www.ypulse.com/post/view/the-10-luxury-brands-millennials-most-want-to-own (last accessed 05/03/2019).

harass women – often predominantly women with a high number of followers and usually coming from a minority or marginalised group. They bombard these women with misogynistic abuse, which ranges from harassment, threats of physical abuse or sexual assault, attempting to exercise their assumed position of power over women, while hiding behind a computer screen. As we discussed in Chapter 4, while many online shooters started out in front of a computer screen, their abuse eventually translates into real life, leading to fatal consequences. Online misogyny is particularly virulent because it is used as a silencing strategy, and it is conveniently ignored as a phenomenon – often by Facebook and Twitter administrators themselves. In a poll conducted across eight countries, the *New Statesmen* reported that approximately 23 per cent of women had experienced online abuse, ranging from 16 per cent in Italy, to 33 per cent in the United States (that's one in three women).[6]

Another research study reported in the *Guardian* revealed that, internationally, more than 200,000 aggressive tweets which contained the words 'slut' and 'whore' were sent over a period of three weeks around the end of April, to 80,000 people.[7] This shows the extent to which online misogyny is able to thrive on social media. What is most surprising is that the perpetrators of this online misogyny range from teenage boys to married men with children. This just shows that male entitlement runs across the board, through all ages, and can't simply be reduced to immaturity and something we grow out of.

A number of women have written about unsolicited dick pics, mainly in blogs and articles. Although indecent or explicit

6   www.newstatesman.com/2017/11/social-media-and-silencing-effect-why-misogyny-online-human-rights-issue (last accessed 05/12/2018).

7   www.theguardian.com/technology/2016/may/25/yvette-cooper-leads-cross-party-campaign-against-online-abuse (last accessed 05/12/2018).

exposure is not something new, it has become more prevalent in the digital age, particularly on dating platforms such as Tinder and Match – 49 per cent of women received an unsolicited dick pic on Match.[8] Sending unsolicited dick pics happens via email and other forms of online communication: not only on dating apps. But there is something particularly insidious about sending the picture on Snapchat. Men know it will be permanently erased after 24 hours – unless someone screenshots the picture, which you will be alerted to, men can get away with violating people's personal online space. But *why* do men send unsolicited dick pics? – 'unsolicited' being the key word here. Sending unsolicited pictures reinforces power dynamics – it makes them *feel* like the man. In many ways, it is a sexually aggressive act, much like catcalling on the street, an act through which men attempt to assert their masculinity and desirability.

A digital silver lining?

We've seen that in many ways, social media and the digital realm provides an outlet for toxic masculinity to thrive: an arena where men can exercise the control they are granted in society, trolling women when they feel power slipping away from them. However, traditional, toxic, or stereotypical notions of masculinity have been challenged as a result of social media and the online world. For example, the members of K-Pop band Bangtan Sonyeondan (BTS), have brightly coloured hair, colourful clothing, pretty faces, often wear make-up, and seamlessly transition in their image between what is seen as masculine and feminine in a way that is exciting and transformative. It is particularly powerful when it comes to challenging stereotypical East Asian mascu-

---

8   https://torontosun.com/life/relationships/why-do-men-send-unsolicited-d-pics
(last accessed 05/03/2019).

linity, which is presented through popular culture and film as associated with either martial arts and fighting, or being nerdy and geeky.

Kehinde Wiley, an African-American artist, re-imagines Black masculinity through delicate portraits of Black men in confident, bold poses, set against colourful, flamboyant and floral backdrops; a particularly outstanding piece is his portrait of former United States President Barack Obama against a leafy, floral backdrop. Photographer Joseph Barrett, in his series *The Male Gaze*, uses a collection of intimate portraits of his friends that attempt to show each person removed from gender stereotypes that surround them. Barrett says in a feature with *Hunger TV*, 'I think it is necessary for people to see photographs without implications of gender and sexual orientation.' The Netflix series, *Queer Eye*, is a fantastic example of subverting traditional masculinity, in particular through the lens of sexuality. The show follows five men, who are gay, and in each episode are given a subject, usually a man, whose life they have to transform with their 'queer' touch – improving the man's sense of dress, style, well-being and self-confidence, moving them away from the traditional masculine image of a man who does not care about self-maintenance or appearance. The opening episode shows the five men transform the life and self-esteem of fifty-seven-year-old Tom, mechanic/trucker, from Georgia, who initially says 'you can't fix ugly' about himself all the time. They share moments of closeness and reflect on dark times, and in the end, Tom is very open-minded, crying and revealing that he had developed a close friendship with them. There are also a number of blogs such as *Woke Daddy* and *The Good Men Project* that offer alternative, progressive discussions on masculinity.

The positives indicate that there is a silver-lining in the dark cloud of misogyny and toxic masculinity, in particular in the digital age, however, the challenge is that the positives tend to occur individually on a personal level. For real change to happen, challenging toxic masculinity needs to be part of a collective cultural and social transformation and shift in consciousness.

Chapter 8

Slamdunk the funk: Masculinity and sport

I played competitive basketball at the national level from the age of 14. I got into it after I broke my arm playing football, following a series of various other early injuries, and a timely teenage growth spurt that eventually led my father to strongly advise that I try a different sport. My childhood friend on our estate had bought a basketball, and we began playing – with no court, or even a hoop – passing the ball and playing dribbling games. We eventually got some hoops up on our estate and started playing at our secondary school; we put together the school's first basketball team. As I grew older, I went on to pursue basketball seriously, competing at the national level, winning a few national titles and trophies along the way that now sit rusting somewhere in the storage cupboard at my parent's place.

Basketball connected and surrounded me with such amazing people, such amazing boys and men who were tall, athletic, strong, yet compassionate, caring, and empathetic. The kind of men who in one breath would tease you about your wonky hairline because your Dad had spent two hours cutting your hair with a pair of scissors (the cost of a barbershop haircut x 5 boys was really expensive), but would also have deep discussions and help you figure out who you were and what you want to do in life. The kind of boys and men who become life-long best friends, and ended up being the best man at your wedding or the godfather to your children. However, this nostalgic reflection on basketball isn't to say that it was always ideal, or easy; there were lots of challenges, from getting beat up in the changing rooms to the trashy language used alongside the pressure to conform. The deepest challenges were always personal. For me, this challenge took place in 2005. It was the season after we had won two national titles – the championship and the cup – and a string of other competitions at the local level. It was a great year for basketball. I felt like I was on my way to making a career in this sport; my dreams were beginning to realise. I had started to draw the attention of Division 1 and 2 colleges and university scouts in America, phone calls trickled in from people with accents we only heard in movies and TV shows, mentioning trials, camps and scholarships, convincing my parents that sending their son to a strange and foreign land was worth the risk. That summer passed. Many of my basketball friends and teammates moved forwards with their careers, some signed professionally in Europe and around the world, some accepted scholarships from colleges in America, but I remained in London, situation unchanged. I continued playing basketball. And though I played, I felt an emptiness growing inside of me; a chasm of epic proportions. The light was dimming, the fire was dwindling, the passion was starting to die.

During the warm-up of a game, my coach noticed that there was a difference in my step; less energetic, less purposeful; without direction, and asked me 'You don't seem yourself. You're playing, but what do you *want* from this?' For the first time ever, I did not have an answer. I had always wanted to play professional basketball, ever since I picked it up on the estate. I had reached the point where I could not imagine my life without it, and would often proclaim that basketball was life. But at that moment, it was no longer life, it was a stranger; a grey shadow lurking in the darkness, following me home. I did not want to play professional basketball; I did not even want to play basketball. In fact, I didn't want to do anything. I wanted to go to sleep for a long time. I wanted to sit in the dark. I wanted to be left alone. I wanted to disappear, to be away, far away, anywhere but here. I was profoundly suffering inside, and not only did I not know why; I did not even know.

I stood next to my coach holding back the tears that swelled beneath my eyes. My coach sent me back out to the court, unaware of how I felt. I was depressed. I played the rest of the game with heavy feet, and a heavier heart, fighting back the tears that were inside and despite all my efforts, we lost. It was that year the dream died.

The 'strong sportsman'

Professional male athletes are often seen as the apex of men's masculinity. They are tall, muscular, in peak physical condition, competitive, and usually extremely wealthy – attributes that are often deemed as desirable for manhood. Athletes are largely influential in shaping the mentality and development of young men, which can be both a positive and a negative.

On 17 February 2018, then NBA basketball All Star Shooting Guard of the Toronto Raptors, Demar DeRozan, originally from Compton, Los Angeles, tweeted 'This depression get the best of me . . .' I am a long-standing, avid NBA fan. I had watched Demar DeRozan since he was first drafted into the NBA by the Toronto Raptors in 2009. I had seen him, over the years, develop from a relatively unknown rookie to franchise athlete, and Mr 'I am Toronto.' What was also beautiful to witness was the development of DeRozan's friendship with fellow superstar teammate,

Kyle Lowry – in a candid interview, they stated they had a bond that was 'beyond friendship'. They publicly shared vulnerability and closeness to one another: something that not many male professional athletes allow themselves to do. DeRozan was always mild-mannered, friendly and had a smile on him. So, many people were shocked and taken aback at his revelation of depression.

But that's the deceptive thing about depression and mental health more generally when it comes to sportsmen, who are people that we view as 'tough' – it is very hard to detect that they may be suffering when we see them on the pitch or on the court, acting 'strong'. We also often assume that their wealth excludes them from having problems or mental health issues like the rest of us. Later in an interview with *Slam* magazine, DeRozan elaborated on his tweet saying,

> it's one of them things that no matter how indestructible we look like we are, we're all human at the end of the day . . . we all got feelings . . . it gets the best of you, where (at) times everything in the whole world's on top of you.[1]

DeRozan's admission of depression received a lot of support from fans, including myself, who felt closely connected to his struggles and his story because of their own experiences. It also prompted other NBA players to come forward with their struggles with mental health, such as Washington Wizard Guard, Kelly Oubre, whose family was uprooted because of the Hurricane Katrina tragedy. He said:

> I can definitely relate to it all . . . I'm really good at keeping a poker face because when I was growing up my dad always

---

1 www.slamonline.com/archives/demar-derozan-addresses-depression-tweet (last accessed 05/12/2018.

told me 'don't let anybody see you weak.' Nobody sees that I'm weak, but deep down inside I am going through a lot. Hell is turning over.

NBA All Star and 2016 NBA Champion, Cleveland Cavalier's forward, Kevin Love, had to leave a game due to anxiety and panic attacks. And later wrote – in an article for *The Player's Tribune* titled, 'Everyone Is Going Through Something' – that the panic attack was his first one, he did not previously even know if they were even real, but how going to therapy transformed his outlook on mental health. Talking about their issues did not make the players seem like any less of a man, or less masculine. Rather, they gained a lot of respect from it, and support, and were able to effect change. The National Basketball Association later appointed its very first director of mental health and wellness – an example of change on a structural level. Tender moments of vulnerability from elite NBA players, whose average height and weight is 6ft 7in and 220lbs (99/100kg) – the average height of an American male is 5ft 9in – and are among the peak in strength and physicality, destroys the suggestion that a man has to be strong; and that men are weaker if they are emotional or vulnerable.

Tottenham Hotspurs and English International Danny Rose, in an interview leading up to the 2018 World Cup, revealed his bout with depression, saying it often left him unable to get out of bed in the morning. Rose adds, 'It led me to seeing a psychologist and I was diagnosed with depression, which nobody knows about.'

Community, Competition and Divides

There is an inherent level of competition that may be a societal effect of being a man. – Jordan S

Masculinity does not manifest the same across all sports. It is largely influenced by the culture of what is acceptable within that sport. Though there are norms around 'acceptable' masculinity across all sports, each sport has its own cultural 'rituals', and strengths as well as challenges when it comes to the players and fans.

Football is a global sport that has brought people together from all different nations and cultures across the world. Football 'hooliganism' is a term used to describe aggressive, violent and/ or disorderly behaviour by the fans of a particular team – usually rivals – aimed at the fans of the opposing team. The act of football 'hooliganism' is often a way for men to form camaraderie and bonds, experience excitement and an adrenaline rush, while creating and performing their constructed masculine identity around the sport. The classic independent film *Green Street* (2005), provided insight through a nuanced depiction of the realities of football 'hooliganism'; each of the men had various careers, including the role of PE teacher, and we watched how in-group activity and bonds slowly formed between the men. It was very much like the kind of masculinity portrayed in *Fight Club*; a desire to belong somewhere. Sports can provide men with a community.

While sports can provide men with a sense of community and a place to form bonds, they can also be an arena for divisiveness. In 2018, the Democratic Football Lads Alliance, whose members have links to the far right, organised a fascist march. Their organiser claimed they were protesting 'returning jihadists' and 'AWOL migrants'. Their march was blocked off by anti-fascist and feminist protestors.

Lecturer in Australian studies, Robert Hogg, writes 'Contact sports like rugby need to be recognised for what they are: ritualised and repetitive displays of hypermasculinity, staged by men for men.'[2] Hoggs distinguishes between contact and non-contact sports, and how that relates to masculinity. Sports such as rugby, football, and American football (NFL), have been accused of issues around hypermasculinity and aggression, both in the sport and outside of it. For Hoggs, non-contact sports such as basketball, tennis, cricket, or athletics, are not always confronted with these same issues.

However, contact or non-contact, a competitive energy can manifest in violence and aggression when it comes to men's sports. For example, women take their sports just as seriously and, in many cases, are just as competitive as men, but we don't see violence break out during a match or game as often. Aggression in sports often has a ripple effect on the fans. The 'malice at the palace' incident in 2004 saw players of the Indiana Pacers and Detroit Pistons get into a mass brawl, with players, as well as the fans in the stand. It was brutal. Following this, the then NBA commissioner, David Stern, instituted a strict policy, including professional dress code, more security and limited sale of alcohol at games. The new rules gradually effected a shift in the openness and expression of the athletes as well as the fans; many players, such as NBA All Star Russell Westbrook, became style icons, wearing bright colours and tightly fitted clothing that would normally be considered feminine or emasculating.

In the article, 'Whether teams win or lose, sporting events lead to spikes in violence against women and children,' writer Melanie Pescud, a visiting fellow at the Australian National University, says across all sporting events, nationally and internationally, such as the World Cup, AFL Grand Final and Melbourne Cup, and even smaller events such as the Calgary Stampede (rodeo – in Canada), men are more aggressive and

---

2 https://theconversation.com/masculinity-and-violence-the-men-who-play-rugby-league-14111 (last accessed 05/12/2018).

violent towards their partners, and children, sometimes by up to 40 per cent.[3] Some have linked it to drinking culture and increased alcohol consumption around game time, but all of this has to be considered alongside a culture where male aggression and competitiveness thrives.

Diversity in sports

Sports face challenges when it comes to diversity, inclusion and representation. Sports such as tennis and rugby, are considered to be suburban, middle-class sports, largely made up of white players, whereas a sport like football is more diverse, considered to be a working-class sport when it comes to its fans and the backgrounds of the players. David Whelan, writing for *Vice Sports*, claims,

> Across the last 28 Grand Slams, only one non-white player has competed in a men's final – Jo-Wilfried Tsonga at the Australian Open in 2008. Currently, there are only two black players in the Men's top 50 and only 1 from Asia. Since the ATP Tour began in 1990, only Michael Chang and Tsonga have won any of the ATP 1000 Master events. Statistically, it's more likely you'll get into Harvard School of Law than see a male Black or Asian player win a Slam in your lifetime.[4]

While a sport like football is much more diverse in terms of the makeup of teams, this has not always translated to acceptance and inclusion. A Sky Data Poll in 2019 revealed that some 71 per

---

3 http://theconversation.com/whether-teams-win-or-lose-sporting-events-lead-to-spikes-in-violence-against-women-and-children-99686 (last accessed 05/03/2019).

4 David Whelan, *Vice Sports*, https://sports.vice.com/en_uk/article/pg5njm/does-tennis-have-a-race-problem (last accessed 19/03/2019).

cent of Black, Asian and ethnic minority fans have had racist abuse directed at them at least once a match.[5] The players, as well as their fans, have also shared their experiences of racism during games.

Competitive sports desperately need to improve on their representation treatment of gay athletes and sports figures. There are very few players who are openly gay, across all sports, while organised sports, even in school environments, are an area that is considered alienating to gay people.[6] This begs the question of just how much this is influenced by a culture of a 'testosterone, teasing, and communal showers', according to France International and Chelsea striker Oliver Giroud who says it is impossible to be openly homosexual in football and that football is a long way away from accepting gay players. Cyd Zeigler, writing for OutSports.com, cites examples of gay players who are out and have had successful careers such as soccer player Robbie Rogers in 2013, who later went on to win the MLS cup with LA Galaxy or former NBA player Jason Collins of the Brooklyn Nets, and more. Regardless of progress that has been made, there could always be more representation and acceptance, among the players and the fans, for the LGBTQ community in sports. A Stonewall research report in 2018 found that 58 per cent of British people think it's important anti-LGBT language is challenged at live sporting events, while only 25 per cent felt confident to call out derogatory remarks,[7] showing that attitudes are shifting but people need sporting environments in which they are confident to do and say more.

---

5   Geraint Hughes, Sky Data Poll. https://news.sky.com/story/sky-data-poll-90-of-football-fans-have-witnessed-racism-at-a-game-11631891 (last accessed 19/03/2019).
6   www.equality-network.org/our-work/policyandcampaign/out-for-sport/the-facts.
7   www.stonewall.org.uk/news/stonewall-reveals-brits-find-it-hard-challenge-anti-lgbt-abuse-sport.

Emotion and vulnerability in sports

Men expressing intimacy and closeness . . . We're not taught how to do that in Western society. – Jordan H

While competitive sports can encourage an atmosphere of aggression, sport is also one of the few spaces where men have been able to comfortably express themselves, and engage and connect with one other. Furthermore, it is one of the few, rare spaces where men can openly show emotional vulnerability and cry and not find that it compromises their identity as a man, or even how others perceive them. Here are some classic sport tear-jerker and athlete crying moments that everyone did or can still relate to:

- Gareth Southgate missed a penalty against Germany at the Semi-final of the Euro 96 Football tournament
- Michael Jordan during his Basketball Hall of Fame Enshrinement Speech – if this seems unfamiliar to you, you will probably recognise it in the alternative form of the Michael Jordan crying meme. This speech is the origin of the internet frenzy
- LeBron James winning the 2016 NBA Finals, and bringing the promised championship to his hometown team the Cleveland Cavaliers; 'Cleveland, this is for you'
- Tennis superstar Roger Federer after beating Pete Sampras, after losing to Rafael Nadal, after winning the Tennis World USA, the Australian Open, Wimbledon – basically, Federer cries a lot (and this is touching), so much so that there is even a 'Top Ten crying moments of Roger Federer' video highlights on YouTube

- Practically every male athlete at the Olympics who wins, or loses and comes agonisingly close to winning

There are so many more examples of male athletes crying across different sporting competitions. Sports are often seen as a noble and just cause for men, in society, where otherwise this level of emotional expression would be castigated. Just imagine a man crying at work after the successful completion of a project or crying after having lost a client.

In the early 2000s, my basketball team had made it to the National Cup finals at Crystal Palace, the then national sports centre for basketball. We lost – a mere margin of six points, against a team that we had beaten twice during the regular season. After the game, we remained in the changing room. I was in tears. So were several of my teammates. The sacrifice, the emotion, the pain, it was normal, it was understood. This wasn't the first national title we had won or lost, nor was it the first competition, or even a single game, that we had cried at after the result. Looking back, I cannot think of any other instance where we would all be crying like that. I had not witnessed a group of young men crying like this, especially in a way that is accepted, not even at a funeral. The bonds that we formed in our team, and across the sport, allowed us to express ourselves and connect in ways we would not have otherwise been able to.

Male vulnerability and emotion in sports can have a radical and progressive influence on how masculinity is viewed in wider society. Sport is a powerful conduit for change, not just on a political level, but also on a personal level. For masculinity in sport to change, it needs to begin at the grassroots, the local and community level, and then work its way up. As much as coaches nurture the physical and athletic development of their athletes and players, they should also be putting as much consideration into the emotional development, by helping the player to be able to deal with competition, and adversity, both in the sporting world and outside of it too. This will hopefully have a wider impact on the way the fans of the sport engage and what behaviours they accept on and off the sporting field. If this is also combined with support from the top end of the sporting world, the professional teams, the brands and the institutions, it will change everything we have seen in sports so far.

Conclusion

Man in the mirror: Transgression and transformation

Patriarchy can seem ubiquitous. It can feel all consuming, all encompassing; controlling every part of your life, from the way you see yourself to the way you see others, from your relationships and friendships, to familial ties, from identity to opportunities and experiences. Yet at the same time, it can also seem invisible. Often, the weight of patriarchy is heavy, but when you've been carrying a weight for so long, you forget what it feels like to be without that weight. You start to then think that carrying that weight is normal, rather than thinking of what you could do to put that weight down – or how much freer you could be without it.

From an early age, you are told about everything to do with masculinity, with boyhood and manhood, as if it is normal, natural: absolute, even. We are told that it is the way it is supposed to be, that any other way has and never will be possible. As we grow up, we read, we experience life and meet people who change our perceptions, and become more informed about the different cultures and different historical periods. We become inquisitive, we start to ask questions and find some answers, but those answers only lead to more questions, and then more questions after that. But as the questions become more and more complex, you find yourself not necessarily finding the answers to everything but growing more as a person, changing and becoming more comfortable with who you are to be and how you see the world.

The system and ideology of patriarchy informs both men and women about masculinity, about boyhood, manhood, and what it means to be a man. But it is a system, an ideology, that is created and maintained by people, and so, it can also be changed, transformed, and eradicated, by people too. However, it takes people who are firstly aware of the problem, and are conscientious and passionate enough to be able to do something about it. Not only for their own sake, but for the sake of others too. One of my biggest motivations for writing this book about masculinity was just how much I would have loved to read a book like this when I was a teenage boy coming to terms, and often struggling, with my own masculinities. I remember the many nights I spent in tears, writhing in pain, submerged by emotional turmoil, on the verge of self-destruction, depressive, or worse, angry and full of rage, at the world, at myself. I was angry without a soul to lament to; feeling the burden I carried was too heavy, and that there was something wrong with me because, unlike the other men in my life, or so it seemed, I was not strong enough to carry that burden. I think about the years I would have saved if I had someone to talk to, to open up to, and have the kind of conversations that are evoked in this book, so that I could understand myself better, and unlearn the things about my masculinity that I had been conditioned to believe were true; that there wasn't something wrong with *me*, there was something wrong with *it*.

I think about how there is much more pressure on young people today to obtain the often unrealistic standards and expectations that society sets for them; how hyper-exposed they are to negativity, through bombardment of content from mainstream and social media, and just how crucial and important a book like this could be to a young boy or man who is questioning his own male identity – who may be feeling conflicted because he cries or is vulnerable, feeling like less of a man for it, on the verge of having a breakdown that could lead to depression, or suicide. Could books like this help to support and validate our existence? A mother, an aunt, a sister, or girlfriend may be worried about the boy or man in their life, whatever their relationship may be, and want to gain a deeper understanding on the male experience, which is so rarely written about beyond the patriarchal stereotypes, and give them support. Or the young girl or woman, growing into herself, trying to understand the system of patriarchy that surrounds her and dominates her life, trying to understand the links between current brutality and brutality experienced by women, generations before hers. Books like this need to exist in this era because the system of patriarchy must be dismantled; the cracks in the patriarchal system are beginning to appear to more and more people, and if we are to ever live in a truly equal world, then we must all do the work.

Through my many years' experience working with boys, young men and older men too, from work in schools, colleges and universities to youth centres, basketball courts and libraries, working with at-risk boys, ex-offenders, young offenders, excluded students, pupil referral units, and those with mental health issues, as well as my personal experience of masculinity and patriarchy, struggling through boyhood and into manhood, I've made a list of ten suggested courses of action. These can be undertaken on an intrapersonal level and on an interpersonal level, a local and community level, to help create a radically new and transformative vision of masculinity, removed from patriarchal stereotypes that plague us today. Here are ten suggestions:

Let go of anger: A lot of boys and young men carry an internal 'me against the world' burning rage and anger that only intensify as they grow older and it is left unresolved. This feeling can be at its most intense during teenage years from 13 to 19, and can carry on or be triggered during a particular stage or event in our male adulthood. Anger is often the default emotion for men, not becomes it comes easier or more naturally, but largely because men are told that they are not emotional, and anger itself is not seen as an emotion. The anger turns into violence, which becomes the main language of expression. I recall spending much of my teenage years angry at the world, at everything around me, and sometimes at myself, and not really knowing why. The majority of the time the anger was contained within myself, but the few times it was released, it was destructive – sometimes that destruction felt cathartic, however it brought little to no solution to the anger. Looking back, I cannot recall a specific reason why I was so angry: I just remember the intensity of the emotion. In order to let go of the anger, we have to first acknowledge that it is there and that it is destructive. The next step is to control it and find an outlet for it.

Every man should own a diary (or journal): to write down their thoughts, feelings, anxieties, experiences (this is different to a diary for goals and objectives), as often as possible, either daily or weekly. In the absence of therapy, or having someone to open up and talk to (especially someone outside of an intimate relationship – your partner is not your therapist), taking the first step towards this can feel like a giant leap. Writing down the way you feel can be a way to communicate to yourself positively, and can often alleviate the tension and the rage of a traumatic experience that is often repressed until it resurfaces. It's ironic how men are socialised to believe that diaries are feminine or girly, when it in fact can change our lives for the better. There are many proven benefits of keeping a diary or journaling your thoughts and feelings such as becoming more mindful and developing emotional intelligence. Professor James Pennebaker, of the University of Texas, who researches the effects of writing on immune functioning, explains that writing helps to add structure and organisation to feelings of anxiety. And as men are less likely to open up than women are, writing in a diary or journal is a way to still open up about your feelings, but maintain the privacy of not speaking to anyone at all.

The responsibility of men: Men (including younger men) must hold themselves and other men accountable for the ways in which they benefit from male privilege and patriarchy, and actively work to change that: ultimately, men must work to change other men. Growing up in my Congolese community, I remember that the men used to gather and provide interventions for any issue involving another man; whether it was domestic, personal, financial, a funeral, and so forth, there would be a group gathering, where men were given advice and support, but most importantly, the need to change and grow was highlighted. I rarely see this happen today in our communities. As communities become more fractured and dispersed, an element of responsibility of care for other people has waned in the modern era. Men are intervening less and less in clear cases of misogyny or abuse. Perhaps a part of it is fear, but a part of it is certainly to do with a desire to hold on to their slice of the patriarchal pie. We can only change this by holding each other accountable.

Male support groups: Some years ago, a few of my guy friends and I would meet at a café on Saturday afternoons for lunch. It began organically as a result of two of us bumping into each other, realising we lived in the same area and went to the same café spot. Then, we called a few of our other friends to join us as the weeks and months passed. Eventually, it got to the stage where there was eight to ten of us each afternoon. We spoke about everything, from our jobs and careers, to family, to sports, to relationships and break ups, and mental health. Sometimes it was comedic, other times it was deeply personal. We kept this up for the best part of two years, and eventually, as some of us moved away or had other commitments, the numbers dwindled. After we stopped meeting, a friend of mine who attended reached out to say thank you for inviting him every Saturday. He said how he was going through a low point in his life where he really struggled with his mental health and depression, and that those regular meet ups gave him something to look forward to. I had no idea about this while we were all meeting up; he always appeared jovial, loud and enthusiastic. It made me realise just how much, even with our closest friends, we can be oblivious to their mental health struggles and personal battles, but also, just how important community is; a place where we can come together to laugh and lament.

The importance of male friendship/support groups is severely underrated. Men are often accused of having superficial friendships that are centred around sex or sports, but in actual fact, men's friendships go much deeper: they just don't necessarily manifest in the same way that women's friendships do. Men can open up, much like anyone, but that largely depends on there being the kind of space that is free of judgement, but also not solely focussed on 'opening up' or mental health, which can feel intimidating. If you are a man in a male friendship group, see how this works for you. Try to create and cultivate the kind of space where you feel comfortable with each other, whether you are laughing or crying. You'll be surprised at just how many men are actually looking for and in need of such spaces and groups like this without realising it.

Language: *Masculinity or Masculinities* – language has a profound influence on the way that we see the world. As humans, we give names to things, and those things are either objects, or expressions and ideas. And in so naming, we provide a means to share that idea or thought with others. Rather than just talking about masculinity, we should try to pluralise the idea of masculinity, referring to it as 'masculinities', in order to portray that the male identity is not singular; that being a man happens in many ways – it is complex, multifaceted, fluid, dynamic and ever changing. This recognition of 'masculinities' has long existed in academic circles since the late 80s/early 90s, with academics such as R. W. Connell who we discussed in Chapter 1. However, it has not yet caught on in the public sphere when we discuss masculinity.[1] We can use language that fosters growth, and encourages and reinforces notions of positive and complex versions of masculinity and manhood that are transformative. The powerful role that language plays also means making a concerted effort to challenge widespread misogynistic and sexist language that normalises gender stereotypes and divides.

Consent education: Young people should be taught about consent as part of sex education. We shouldn't only be taught about protection and safety, pregnancy and STI prevention, but about consent – saying yes or no, understanding the pressures that influence our choices; ensuring girls or boys and women

---

1   I realise, also, that I spent the majority of this book referring to it as *masculinity* rather than *masculinities*, the reason is that for many readers this will be an introduction/starting point to the conversation, and so it's important to meet people where they are at. And then move the conversation forwards.

or men do not feel pressured to have sex or feel like they cannot revoke consent, and educating boys and men on the fact that they are not entitled to girl's bodies. No Means No Worldwide – a global rape prevention organisation whose mission is to end sexual violence against women and children – introduced a programme in Kenya teaching girls self-defence and boys about positive masculinity. There was a 51 per cent decrease in incidents of rape, 46 per cent reduction of pregnancy-related school dropouts, and 73 per cent of boys intervened to prevent assault. If we are taught that rape is always the rapist's fault and taught to understand the complexities of sexual consent, victim blaming will be challenged, and as proven with the No Means No campaign, we will see positive effects.

Talk Zones: with the prevalence of suicide being so high in men, particularly between the ages of 18–34, safe spaces called 'Talk Zones' should be introduced. These are safe, public spaces where someone can offer to listen or talk to someone who may be going through something. In Zimbabwe, they ran the trial of the 'Friendship Bench' where mental health patients spoke with their therapist or care worker out, in public, on these benches, and this was found to have positive effects on their mental health. A similar strategy rolled out to the general UK public – particularly in metropolitan cities such as London, where people have very little time to stop and talk to each other or can feel alone surrounded by people – via benches or marked out areas, can also have a positive effect on the mental health of that area or community. Men are being encouraged to open up more, but it is very difficult to do so, as you may feel you are a burden on those around you, or, because repressing your emotions is all you've ever known. It can often be easier to talk about your problems to a stranger. Therapy can be difficult to access because of financial circumstances or lack of local authority and community services available (due to cuts in services, as discussed in Chapter 2). Talk Zones could be part of an important cultural shift, helping people to engage in new ways, potentially leading to significant long-term positive consequences.

Parent/Carers: Through the guise of 'boys will be boys', boys are often raised with a greater sense of entitlement than girls. There is so much more expectation and responsibility placed on girls to be mature, to be good, to 'behave', than there is for boys. There needs to be an equal level of expectation and responsibility placed on boys to be mature and to grow. If parents/carers have conversations with boys at a younger age that allows them to understand patriarchy and the expectations placed on their manhood by society, they may be better placed to cope with it long before they experience all aspects of it, understanding that they should not have to adhere to it or accept it as absolute or even true. After all, as the saying by Frederick Douglass goes, 'it is easier to build strong children than to repair broken men.'

Reading: is one of the most transformative tools that can be used to awaken one's consciousness. I believe that every boy or man should read feminist literature and texts that enlighten them about patriarchy and masculinity, as well as women's lived experiences, so that they are at least aware about gender inequality in society. Educational institutions should be supporting this. As boys and men, we should feel encouraged to read more novels by women authors and novels with women protagonists. Often stories which are centred around the worlds of women can help us to conceive of a radically different society where our identity as men is the dominant one. A lot of the young boys I work with are either disinterested in reading or claim to only be interested in non-fiction books – which is where feminist texts or books on gender inequality could be made part of school curriculums. But reading novels and fiction can also help to expand the imagination, and encourage us to develop empathy, as we are drawn to the character and story of a person we would not have otherwise known. Reading transformed me as individual: as a boy, through to being a teenager, to being a man. I accidentally came across literature such as *Will To Change, We Real Cool, The God of Small Things, The Handmaid's Tale, The Bell Jar, I Know Why The Caged Bird Sings* during the most turbulent stages of my masculine identity. I do not think I would have been able to liberate myself from the constraints of patriarchal conditioning had I not read these books (and I certainly would not have been able to write about it either). We should also read literature and books by other men whose identities and experiences go beyond the stereotypical masculine expectations; stories that tell us more about men's personal experience and normalise male empathy.

Love: Men need love. Men need love from other men, not just from women, or their partners. Men need intimate, non-sexual love; a love that goes beyond the expectations placed on their manhood. Often men only feel that they have a place in this world when they can fulfil what is expected of them as a man. As we have discussed throughout, patriarchy benefits men, but it can also equally destroy them. Men need love to overcome destructive feelings, and they need love in order to feel that their life is worth living. Men have to be comfortable with saying 'I love you' to other men, without adding 'bro', 'man' or 'mate', to make it more acceptable or without adding 'no homo' or 'pause', which reduces men expressing love to other men to a question of sexuality. Love and acceptance from ourselves and from those around us makes us comfortable in our own skin.

We cannot face any problems that exist unless we are confronted by them and in turn confront them; unless we inform and educate ourselves as well as unlearn toxic behaviours, and talk to each other about what those problems are. But that education and the subsequent course of action we take requires boldness and it requires courage. It is not enough to know, we must also *do*. It requires us to stand in the face of adversity and dare to say what is unpopular, dare to say what might remove us of our privilege – as men, dare to say what might isolate or ostracise us, but ultimately say it with the full belief that we are using our knowledge to benefit ourselves, our loved ones, our society and community, and to a wider degree, humanity. Whether we are in the barbershop on a Saturday afternoon, waiting in line when someone makes a comment that is sexist or homophobic (and aims to disguise it as 'banter'), or in the locker/changing room after gym or sports, or in the playground at lunch time or in the club, and one of your friends grabs a girl and touches her inappropriately, we should have the courage to speak out on it. But equally, have the courage to educate ourselves and others when we slip up, empathise and be there for those who need it – and always take the time to extend this empathy and love to yourself.

Masculinity is fluid and ever changing. The system of patriarchy is not permanent – it was created by people as all systems of oppression are, and therefore it can be transformed by people too. The world is changed by people who have a vision for a better way of living, a path that fulfils rather than destroys, that uplifts rather than oppresses, which fills us with joy and hope rather than with anger and sadness. The mask that men have worn for decades, even centuries, has to be fully removed for us to see the true face that lies beneath; once we remove it, we will see that what lies beneath is a reflection of our true selves, however we choose to be.

Resources

Organisations and Charities

Mind: A mental health charity offering information and advice to people with mental health problems, lobbying government and local authorities on their behalf.

YoungMinds: A mental health charity fighting for children and young people's mental health.

Campaign Against Living Miserably (CALM): A male suicide prevention charity.

SurvivorsUK: An organisation offering support to male victims of sexual abuse as well as their friends and family.

Good Lad Initiative: An organisation promoting positive masculinity, delivering workshops and resources to schools, universities and in the workplace.

MenEngage Alliance: A global alliance working with men and boys for gender equality.

GoodNightOut: A campaign working to end harassment in bars, venues, clubs and pubs across the world, delivering training to those working in these areas.

MermaidsUK: A charity and advocacy organisation, supporting gender diverse and transgender youth.

Stonewall: An organisation campaigning for the rights of lesbian, gay, bi and trans people across the UK.

Level Up: A new feminist organisation campaigning in three main areas: schools and work, harassment and violence, media and marketing.

All Out: An organisation focused on political advocacy for the human rights of lesbian, gay, bisexual, and transgender people.

The Consent Collective: An activist organisation helping communities talk about sexual harassment, sexual violence and abuse, working with schools, colleges, universities and employers.

RunnyMede Trust: A race equality think tank intervening in social policy and practice.

The ManKind Project: A global network of non-profit training and education organisations focused on modern male initiation, self-awareness and personal growth.

A Call to Men: A national violence prevention organisation providing training and education for men, boys and communities.

The NAZ project: A sexual health charity dedicated to delivering culturally specific sexual health services to BAME communities.

RESOURCES

NUS I Heart Consent Campaign: Education campaign about consent in universities and colleges across the UK.

Further Reading

bell hooks, *We Real Cool: Black Men and Masculinity* (Routledge, 2003).

bell hooks, *Feminism is for Everybody* (Pluto Press, 2000).

R. W. Connell, *Masculinities* (University of California Press, 2005).

Derek Owusu, *SAFE: On Black British Men Reclaiming Space* (Trapeze, 2019).